CHOOSE LIFE!

*I call the heaven and the earth this day to testify concerning you: I place before you life and death, blessing and curse — **choose life!** so that you and your descendants shall live.*

Devarim 30:19

CHOOSE LIFE!

The Purpose of Creation as the Key to Happiness,
Meaning, Life

(And including ROSH HASHANNAH: *Unveiling the
Purpose of Creation*, a supplemental writing)

by
Rabbi Ezriel Tauber

Written by
Yaakov Astor

2nd Edition
Hardcover ISBN 1-878999-06-0
Softcover ISBN 1-878999-03-6

Shalheves
P.O. Box 361
Monsey, N.Y. 10952
(914) 356-3515

Wholesale Distribution:
Philipp Feldheim Inc.
200 Airport Executive Park
Spring Valley, NY 10977

Feldheim Publishers Ltd.
POB 35002
Jerusalem, Israel

". . . her flashes are like the flashes of fire, the flame of G-d (Shalheves Kah)."
(Shir HaShirim 8:6)

Printed in Israel

CONTENTS

OUTLINE OF TOPICS*

---

*   Three main themes run through *Choose Life!*: Life, the people Israel, and Torah. To facilitate understanding, the following outline can be referenced. Glance at it before reading the book in order to gain a sense of the overall framework, and/or use it to help sort through and review the material once the book has been read.

PREFACE

I am truly humbled and grateful to the Almighty for helping
me publish this book. I also must express my debt of gratitude
to the general public, who have attended the lectures upon
which this book is based. In their merit, *Hashem* has granted
me the insights and original thoughts I delivered at those
lectures. And it is those very thoughts which comprise this
book as well. I am truly indebted.

MAN HAS INVENTED two great tools which give him
access to worlds otherwise hidden from the human eye: the
telescope and microscope. The telescope helps him search
outward to the stars of the universe, while the microscope
helps him probe inward to the universe within. Similarly, there
are two great methods which give one access to knowledge of
self, otherwise hidden from view: realizing how small one is,
and realizing how great one is.

Arrogance, pride, hubris, etc. are human failings where indulgence of self leads to denial of others. To correct this type of human failing, a spiritual telescope is required. Look into the heavens, see what G-d has made — if one does that, how long can he remain boastful? After all, what is man compared to G-d? Not even a drop of water compared to all the world's oceans.

On the other hand, an over-indulgent sense of worthlessness fails humanity as well. When we think that whatever we do does not matter anyway, then it is time to take out a spiritual microscope and probe how much every little act, every little moment is worth.

In my opinion, the more commonly found root of depression and sadness in our day and age is a lack of appreciation for who we are and what we can accomplish. This book therefore is a spiritual microscope. It magnifies the greatness in each of us. And we do need to believe that we are great — not an arrogant, false greatness, but rather an authentic sense of self-worth which is founded upon true awareness of G-d. Knowing how what we do really matters is the secret to well-being, happiness, and everything good.

HAPPINESS, indeed, is an elusive goal, especially in our times. That makes it all the more strange, then, to read that the Torah obligates us to serve G-d joyfully. In fact, failing to do so is counted against us, as the Torah says, "[The bad tidings will come upon you] because you did not serve G-d with happiness and a good heart . . . " (*Devarim* 28:47).

What if one is beset by difficult circumstances beyond control? How can one be joyful then?

However, because G-d obligates us to be happy, He must

also have given us the ability to attain it no matter what our particular circumstances. The question is: What is the magic formula for attaining happiness?

The first thing to understand is that magic has nothing to do with it.

Happiness is a function of knowledge. The Rambam (Maimonides) teaches that, "Love of G-d [and the ensuing satisfaction with life] comes only through knowing Him; in relation to the knowledge, so will be the love . . . Therefore, it is necessary to deepen one's knowledge of G-d as much as possible" (Laws of Repentance 10:6).

Serving G-d without understanding turns everything into a chore. Conversely, any comprehension of G-d's underlying plan can turn even otherwise painful and 'mundane' situations into meaningful, satisfying experiences.

This book is about doing just that: turning the everyday into the uncommon, the meaningless into the meaningful. To do so, it is necessary to attack the big questions in life: What is life? What is the purpose of creation? What is the definition of happiness? What is a human being? What is a Jew?

The true poverty of today's world is that so many people do not know how to answer these questions. Many more do not even know enough to ask. And there is nothing as irrelevant as an answer without a question.

Therefore, if this book does nothing else it would be a success if it only aroused the curiosity to ask the above questions. These questions lead one to grapple with the fundamental principles of life, principles from which love, happiness and everything good sprout.

I have seen lives turned around dramatically because all of a sudden a previously obscure or unknown principle became clear. It can be as simple as that. Yet, too often we fail to address the very things which we need to make the most out of life. "Don't confuse me with the facts" is the all too common attitude. Many of us know of the information, and realize it is at our fingertips, but are afraid to seek it, grab it, believe it, and imbue ourselves with it.

Nevertheless, the "facts" are our most important allies. And they never run away. They are always there for us to utilize whenever we choose to do so. All we have to do is choose to do so.

My hope is that this book will present in an interesting, novel and profound way those very facts, so that we will not be afraid to choose to let them help us learn how to "serve G-d with happiness and a good heart."

The material used in this book has been related in public many times, including a three-day audience with great Torah scholars in *eretz Yisroel.* It was emphasized to them how important their specific feedback was. This resulted in dozens of *haskamas,* which are available upon request.

Furthermore, anyone who has questions and comments concerning this book is encouraged to mail them to Shalheves. The only stipulation is that they be questions of *hashkafa,* not *halacha,* i.e., questions of Torah perspective, not Torah law.

I would like to give heartfelt thanks to all who have allowed me to continue with public lecturing. In particular, I want to thank the volunteers who run the Shalheves program in Monsey, and especially Mr. and Mrs. Gottlieb, who run the Shalheves program in Brooklyn. Also, I want to thank the writer of this book, Yaakov Astor. Due to his efforts, once more an otherwise complex subject has been made widely accessible without detracting from its depth and beauty.

Last, being the most precious, if not for the dedicated support of my dear family, none of this would be possible. May it be *Hashem's* will that we merit to continue with strength and see the Redemption, speedily, in our days.

Ezriel Tauber

WRITER'S INTRODUCTION

A little less than ten years ago, Rabbi Tauber spoke in Jerusalem, as he frequently does when he visits *eretz Yisroel*. As a student enrolled in a *yeshiva* there, I initially felt a little distant from this visiting speaker and his words. About halfway through the thirty-minute lecture, though, I began to realize that his thoughts were striking me somewhere deep inside.

The truth is that by the time I began writing this book, almost ten years later, all that I remembered of that lecture was a cloudy recollection of something related to the idea that business and Torah have an interchangeability about them. (See Part I, chapter 2, subsection *Mysticism in Everyday Life* for how some of the ideas from the tape of that lecture have been incorporated into this book.) The idea that all life is one, that it is not meant to be compartmentalized into separate spheres of secular and religious, is certainly one of the unique, beautiful truths of the Torah outlook. And it is certainly one of the calling cards of Rabbi Tauber's particular emphasis, as well as one of the ideas I personally find so attractive.

However, perhaps even more than the philosophy, that lecture impressed upon me that Torah ideas were meant to be lived. I knew it before, of course, however from that first lecture, Rabbi Tauber struck me as a man who was completely living the Torah truths — whose very life was a testament to those truths. And that is why the impression of seeing him living, breathing, and speaking remained with me even more than his actual words.

When I first began writing for Rabbi Tauber over a year ago it was an experiment for both of us. Others had tried to write for him, but nothing ultimately clicked. And, frankly, I did not know if I could give him what he wanted while at the same time satisfying the need of the reading public.

Then, the very first day I began writing for him, he asked me what ideas I had come up with. At first, I did not know what to answer. Then, all of a sudden, it struck me.

A dialogue.

A dialogue was a way of conveying the abstract Torah ideas in a real-life way. As I briefly explained my idea to him the words seemed to flow naturally. And that is not surprising in light of the above, because Rabbi Tauber had long epitomized to me the ideal that Torah should and could be lived.

His response to my idea for a dialogue was a sincere, "If it is going to be done, that is the way to do it."

And so we began with books based on Rabbi Tauber's lectures on work and marriage. This third book, however, is the foundation of his outlook, of the Torah outlook. It consists of the root ideas upon which the first two books are the branches.

Understanding this book, therefore, is bound to yield a wide-ranging, self-replenishing well of immediate, practical applications. The hope is that *Choose Life!* will help the reader become a creative yet responsible user of Torah principles, so that he or she can make his or her own life a living testament to the Torah of the living G-d.

Writing a dialogue is an odyssey — it is an epic journey into the unknown. Even the most organized writer cannot know what lies just over the horizon. A character, scene or thought will spring up unexpectedly and suddenly change the course of the dialogue.

Yet, in a dialogue such as this there is a definite agenda: Rabbi Tauber outlines to me exactly what he wants to convey; I attend some of his lectures, listen to his tapes and have a pretty good idea of the destination before I start. Then I introduce the dialogue and let the currents of conversation steer the flow. The result, it is hoped, is an engaging reading experience, which teaches many deep ideas in an easily digestible, pragmatic way.

In addition to the dialogue, though, this book contains sections written in non-dialogue fashion. First, much of Part II of this book is for all intents and purposes an expository writing (while remaining within the framework of the dialogue). Second, there is a supplemental essay on *Rosh HaShannah* toward the end of the book, which capsulizes and extends many of the ideas stated previously. And third, the appendix contains a reprinted article written by S. Ornstein on the hidden codes in the Torah.

These non-dialogue elements are no less readable than the dialogue itself, yet add balance to the overall book, and give people who are partial to a non-dialogue style an opportunity to read Rabbi Tauber's words in a manner more suited to their tastes.

Please note that all transliterated Hebrew words have been italicized, and those not defined in the course of the text have been translated in a glossary in the back.

Finally, please do not hesitate to send in your comments or critiques. Your input helps us make a better publication.

Y.A.

CHOOSE
LIFE!

CHAPTER 1

WHY? WHY? WHY?

W hy? Why? Why?

Why, G-d — if you are listening — did you create me? What is the purpose of life? For G-d's sake, what do you want from me?

David flipped past the next couple of pages in his old diary. His eyes settled on the copy of a clipping he had seen on a university bulletin board:

This life is a test. It is only a test. Had it been a real life you would have been informed where to go and what to do, etc.

Memories of the confusion and loneliness from that period in his life were coming back to him. His diary was serving as a mirror to the past. "Where did it all begin?" he thought. How did he, an educated, modern person ever even admit to the possibility that his ancient religion was really nothing but an outdated relic?

Yes, believing in a G-d was one thing; perhaps there was an all-knowing Being who created the world. That was not too hard to accept. However, to be intrigued with the possible implications so much that he took to studying the Torah, how could he do it? Of course, now he understood, somewhat at least, the depth and beauty of it all, however, before "The Conversation" (as he had labeled that great turning point in his life) what could have persuaded him to even let the possibility enter his mind?

There was Cindy, his non-Jewish girlfriend; there was the feeling he harbored that he was as happy as he ever had been; and there was the inner confidence that he knew enough about the world and Judaism to not think twice about intermarrying. When a Jewish friend asked him about it he answered, "Why not? I like her; is anything else more important? I feel a little badly about it, but am I really losing anything? What am I giving up?"

Of course, the friend had no response, and that only convinced David more that Jewish people who clung to the faith were living in the past. If she were a Jewish girl, fine. If not, also fine.

At least that was the way he used to think, and he still remembered that answer to his friend quite vividly. What then led him to attend a lecture given by a rabbi (and a very religious looking one at that)? In the end, there was only one answer he could come up with: the source of the "trouble" was that nagging question "Why?".

"Why? Why? Why?" ringing in his head would not give him peace. It would be easy to be superficial like many people he knew and never admit the question existed. However, David realized he could never be truly happy without at least addressing that silent inner voice beckoning him to dig beneath the surface.

So he attended the lecture. Why not a lecture by a guru or some other claimant to the mysteries of the universe? Perhaps it was all the fuss some people close to him had made; perhaps it was the consideration that if there was a Creator why would He have given him Jewish parents?

Whatever the reason, it was no big deal, he told himself. Attending this rabbi's lecture was a small concession, a token gesture to appease the voice of his conscience. Once he reconfirmed that Judaism held no answers, then he might try somewhere else, or resign himself — as he basically already had — to living with the conviction that there were just some questions which had no answers.

In any event, he attended the lecture, which he had to admit was not totally uninteresting. The lecturer was a distinguished looking rabbi who made some good points. For reasons he didn't understand, though, David found himself compelled to approach him after the lecture.

A few other people had gathered around the rabbi (ahead of David) to ask their questions. As David began to feel self-conscious, being there without a definite reason, the last of the questioners departed and he was left standing before the rabbi, alone, feeling awkward and having to come up with something to say.

He decided, as he so often did when he was not sure of himself, to be very straight-forward. He briefly told the rabbi about his background, education, career goals and finally the very real possibility of marrying a non-Jew. The latter point he had stated with a mixture of trepidation and defiance, as if almost daring the rabbi to come up with an argument that would persuade him otherwise.

The answer the rabbi did give did not impress him — or at least so he first thought. He told David to imagine that a man came up to him on the street and handed him a sealed envelope. This man told him that in the envelope was the winning ticket to yesterday's million dollar lottery drawing and he was giving it to him for free, no strings attached.

The rabbi then asked David if he would tear the envelope up and throw it in the garbage without even looking, passing off the entire incident as the distorted sense of humor of a crazy man? Or, the rabbi asked, would he at least open up the envelope to take a peek?

"I suppose I'd open it up," David told him.

"So, too," the rabbi continued, "I come to you. The

Jewish religion is an unbroken chain stretching back over 3,300 years, passed on from generation to generation; by going on with your move, do you realize that you are abandoning your faith and in effect breaking the chain?"

"Yes. So what? What does the faith really give me?"

"Ah, the answer to that is what lies inside the envelope. By going ahead with this decision, you are making the choice without knowing what you are abandoning; you are throwing away the envelope without ever opening it up."

David paused and thought for a moment. "That may be true, rabbi," he finally said, "but to learn about my religion takes a little more than just opening up an envelope."

"Yes," he answered, "but in comparison to losing even a million dollars, what you stand to lose by abandoning your heritage is much greater."

David reflected. "If that's true, then, what would you recommend?"

"Pick yourself up and find a school here or in Israel to discover what Judaism is about and what your true roots are."

"I'm not going to go to a school where someone tells me what to do, what to eat, what to wear, and what to think," David asserted.

"It's not like that at all. There are schools for intelligent people just like yourself who go there simply to learn what it is about. Give yourself one month of honest learning. After one month, sit down and analyze your options. If, then, you decide to marry out of the religion, at least you can say that you opened the envelope and peeked inside."

"I suppose it is something to think about, but I don't see what I can gain by it. No one is going to tell me what to do with my life. I have free choice."

"True, no one is going to tell you what to do with your life, but do you really have as much free choice as you think? Choice is something you have only when you fully understand the available options. Until you open the envelope, the second option does not really exist for you."

The rabbi continued: "Your statement just reminded me of the question a young woman once posed to me."

"'I was raised,' she said, 'in a way where I could do anything I wanted. I have been fully committed to observing the Torah for a while now, and I know there is a reason for everything, but it bothers me that there are some things I can't do like I used to.'"

"'What exactly bothers you?' I asked."

"'The fact that I can't dress the way I want to dress,' she said. 'I understand the reasons behind the Torah's laws of modest dress, and intellectually they make sense to me, but it's not the way *I* like to dress. It's just not me.'"

"'Who is the *me*?' I asked her. 'You were born into a non-observant family; your parents placed you in a public school and then sent you to college. Were you ever given an opportunity to really look into your heritage?'"

"'No,' she replied."

"'Since you were a child, you were programmed to live in one way. You grew up, searched on your own, and discovered the beauty of Judaism. Only then did you first gain the option to choose between it and the way you were raised. Your decision to commit to Torah was the first decision made by the real you. Before then, you never even had the opportunity to be you!'

"I knew her well," the rabbi said, "so I knew I could speak strongly to her in that instance. I don't know you, David, but you appear to me to be someone unafraid of the truth: Who are you?" the rabbi asked and then paused for a few long moments. "We all must ask ourselves: Who am I? Who is the capital 'I'? Did I develop myself? Am I not a product of a particular upbringing and society? And if so, don't I owe it to myself to expose myself to a part of me which may be outside the norm of my upbringing?"

"I understand what you are driving at, rabbi," David replied, "but isn't the same true for you, except in reverse? Couldn't someone come to you and say that your parents raised you in the Torah lifestyle, and therefore, you never knew any other way."

"In fact, someone once did, except in a little stronger language. He told me that he pitied me because I never grew up knowing what the world had to offer. He said that my parents took away my free choice.

"'Maybe you could have become a great lawyer,' he told me, 'but they brainwashed you, instead, to become a religious fanatic (to use his terminology). I'm a free person,' he boasted. 'I don't have a guilty conscience driving me *meshuga* and telling me to do this or do that.'"

"What did you answer him?" David inquired.

"I told him, 'I don't have to go to public school to know what the world has to offer. I meet all types of people daily. Furthermore, posters, advertisements, media, communication arts, etc. — all I need to do is drive a car, walk down the street or go to the supermarket to see very well what the world is all about.

"'My parents,' I continued, 'gave me a solid grounding in the Torah lifestyle, a lifestyle which generally goes against the flow of society. I now have two clear options in front of me. I see the world through the eyes of the Torah, and I see the world through the eyes of the average person growing up in this society, which at every turn exposes its viewpoints to anyone who lives in it. *I* have free choice. *I* am fully exposed to both sides.

"'You, on the other hand,' I told him, 'who never had the opportunity to really know what the Torah is all about — you who never opened the envelope — have only one choice.'" The rabbi paused for a moment and then continued. "David," he said, "only by unfettering oneself from the thought patterns of the popular culture is one truly free to develop his own identity."

"I don't claim to be perfect," David replied, "but I try to think for myself."

"A person can be the greatest thinker in the world, but he is not free to choose until he has clear knowledge of both sides. And to you, at this time, Judaism is not a choice because you do not know enough about it to honestly reject it."

"I may not know the Torah, but I have a Jewish awareness."

"A Jew who is ignorant of Torah cannot consider his identity intact. Until relatively recently every Jew, even illiterate ones, were knowledgeable of Torah. Torah knowledge is the essential component of Jewish identity, of your identity. What is your Jewish awareness if you are missing the essence?"

"But from what I know of it," David said, "Torah is very simplistic. It may have been good for Jews in old Europe, but the world is more sophisticated today."

"The important words are 'from what you know of it.' Perhaps it is your understanding of Torah which lacks sophistication."

"Perhaps."

"A Torah by the Creator of heaven and earth is as shallow or deep, and as narrow or broad, as the one who learns it. It is not just Bible stories and a Sunday morning bagels and lox philosophy. You owe it to yourself to broaden your understanding of Torah. And until you do, you are not even free to consider yourself 'you.'"

"That's not what I think."

"But who is the capital 'I'?" the rabbi said. "The whole problem, David, is that you don't realize who you are. Of course, at this point, you probably think I am totally out of line for saying that. However, all I am telling you is to take a peek inside the envelope. Test me and see if I am not just a crazy man coming up to you on the street. Don't throw away the envelope without even opening it. You are intelligent and educated. Put in some honest time learning Torah and empower yourself with choice."

"I will have to think about it," David said just to end the conversation.

On the way home, he convinced himself that the rabbi's argument was flawed. He really didn't understand the situation. Nevertheless, that night he tossed and turned. The next day, he was tired and in a bad mood. When evening came, he spent another restless night trying to fend off the memory of the conversation and its implications. Each time he came up with a rationale and supposedly put the subject to rest it returned to his mind to torment him with a new set of counter-arguments and implications. Finally, after three days and nights, he realized that he had to once and for all repress it or contact the rabbi to find out more.

"Yes. I remember you," the rabbi said, trying to hold

back his surprise over hearing David's voice on the other end of the telephone.

"I've been thinking a lot about what you said," he told the rabbi, "and the bottom line is that I realize I don't know the inner contents of the envelope. However, I am not ready to take a flight to Israel or even go to some local school until you can convince me that there is something of real value inside the envelope."

"That's a tall order," the rabbi said, "to take and fill over the phone."

"I realize that, so if you want I am ready to meet you."

"Fine. Would you be able to come over to my office in, say, two hours?"

"Yes."

"Good. Then I'll expect you. Do you have the address?"

"Yes."

"I look forward to seeing you."

CHAPTER 2

THE TREE OF LIFE

To David, the two hours seemed to take forever. He kept on replaying the questions he would ask and the possible answers he could be given. Just before arriving, however, he realized that the tone of his thoughts was antagonistic, and he admitted that a more honest approach would be to hear the rabbi out without jumping on every detail. He would be cautious yet open, detached yet inquisitive.

The conversation began a little awkwardly, but eventually opened up. After a while, David decided to get to the point.

"Rabbi," he asserted, "the truth is that the only reason I am here is because I can't get the idea of the envelope out of my head. I don't know why it bothers me so much, but it does. I realize you think I should attend a school for a month, but I don't want to at this point. And if I were to ever seriously consider the possibility, why shouldn't I try other religions?"

"You weren't born into them. First, find out about the one you were born into."

"But why not pick and choose from each?"

"Because Torah is a coherent whole which is greater than the sum of its parts. You can't pick and choose from it like a Chinese menu. It is like an engine. Would you take out the carburetor of your car because you didn't understand how it helped the engine run? If it is there, you assume the engine designer put it there for a reason.

"So, too, you cannot pick and choose from the Torah, discarding what you think does not make sense. You have to assume the Designer had a reason for every word and nuance. Therefore, to know what the Torah is you have to see it as a whole, with all its parts intact. Spend a concentrated time learning about it in its entirety from the authentic teachers and original sources, and, then, if you want, see how others compare to it."

"I don't know," David said. "You seem to find a lot of meaning in the Torah, but maybe you are fooling yourself. Maybe you are reading into the Torah more than there is. My opinion is that it is man-made, perhaps by geniuses, but man-made nonetheless."

"And you are entitled to your opinion," the rabbi

responded, "however, how can you say that for sure without ever seriously sitting down and studying Torah?"

"Rabbi," David said with a look of sincerity, "let me ask you to be frank with me. Do you really believe that there once was a great world-wide flood, and all the animals around today survived only because a man named Noah built an ark and actually fit them all in that ark? You don't sound so fanatical or primitive to me. I can't believe you really believe that story."

"Yes. I firmly believe the Torah's account."

"How could it be? Even an ark the size of an aircraft carrier couldn't fit inside of it all the basic species of animals in the world, not to mention enough food to supply them for an entire year. How do you believe any of that stuff?"

"If fifty years ago I insisted that it is possible to take a small, plastic chip and put on it all the information which is contained in the New York City Library — what would you say? You would have laughed at me. You would have called me crazy. Yet, today we see it is possible.

"A computer chip is a mind-boggling, 'miraculous' device made by man," the rabbi said. "If all G-d needed to do was perform a small miracle to make all the animals fit in the ark, why shouldn't I believe it? True, I don't necessarily understand it. However, do you believe that libraries of information can be stored on a computer chip?"

"Yes."

"Do you understand it?"

"No."

"I don't understand it either," the rabbi said, "but why do we believe it, because nowadays we see computers in action. So, too, I see the principles of Torah in action every day — through myself and others. That's how I really know that it is true. You, on the other hand, have not taken a close look at the Torah lifestyle in action for yourself. That is why you have trouble believing what I am telling you. And that is also why I am not telling you to take my word for it, but to learn some Torah in depth so you can find out for yourself."

"I don't know."

"You are at a crucial point in your life. Why not take some time and find out for sure?"

"I suppose the bottom line," David said, "is that I don't want to learn about Judaism or Torah. If I am here for anything, I am only here for one reason: to learn about life."

A smile came across the rabbi's face. "And my answer to you," he said, "is that they are one and the same. The Torah is called a tree of life. It is the root of this world and if you don't grab onto it the results can be disastrous."

"Disastrous? Isn't that an exaggeration?"

"No. Picture it this way," the rabbi said. "You are canoeing down a fast-water river. All of a sudden you are thrown into the surging rapids. Cut loose from the security of the boat, you are out of control and in danger of drowning. Suddenly, while tossing and turning in the waters, you look up and see a tree. You grab for it and hold on with dear life.

"This is like life," the rabbi continued. "Life is a continuous flow of everchanging, surging currents. Fads, philosophies, finances, leaders and governments are in constant flux. Nothing in this world has permanence. The success with which we meet change and adversity is dependent on how true and well-rooted our beliefs are.

"King Solomon said the Torah is a tree of life to those who grab hold of her.[1] That tree is the inner truth of life which does not change. It stands in the middle while the waters of the modern, mundane world rush all about. There are other things in the water which may at first appear to be able to save us from drowning, but when we grab onto them in our moment of need we find out that they were nothing other than dead wood or shallowly-rooted trees.

"No outlook in the long record of mankind has weathered the ebb and flow of history like Torah. It is not just another philosophy, psychology or self-help trend, and it is not just another religion. It is the root of this world, and what you gain by grabbing onto it is not just some transient happiness — you gain life, real life."

The Challenge of Sinai

"Other religions claim to have the answer to life, too," David said. "Why should I accept what the Torah says more than the teachings of other religions?"

"For one reason, other religions are founded on belief; ours is founded on knowledge."

"What do you mean by that?"

"Christianity says their founder conveyed his vision to a small circle of disciples; Islam says Mohammed alone had a revelation and convinced others. What is to prevent someone from thinking that perhaps they deluded themselves or made the whole thing up, and were just good salesmen to generations who were ripe to be fooled? Their supporters will say, 'Well, that's what makes you a believer or not.'

"The Torah says that when G-d wanted to reveal His will to mankind, He left no room for doubt. He personally revealed Himself to *millions* of people at the foot of Mount Sinai! Moses didn't make the sale; the Torah itself tells us he had a speech impediment. The millions of people at Mount Sinai did not 'believe' the vision Moses had; they heard it from G-d themselves.[2]

"The claim of the revelation at Mount Sinai is unique to Judaism, so unique and challenging in fact that Christianity and Islam have to admit that the 'Old' Testament was true at one time. Their claims to be extensions or completions of it are flimsy in light of the fact that they don't even dare say that an equally undeniable revelation happened to them which might have otherwise lent some credibility to the claim that G-d changed or added to His will.

"What about the Eastern religions? They don't lay claim to the Old Testament."

"Right. And that is their limitation. The most significant event since creation was the giving of the Torah on Mount Sinai. Before Sinai, mankind's knowledge of G-d's goal for it was limited to what human intellect could concoct. Sinai changed all that. It was the one undeniable, all-inclusive revelation of G-d's will. That is what made it so necessary for Christianity and Islam to reinterpret the event for their own ends.

"They can reinterpret all they want, though. There was only one Sinai. And there is only one code of life which G-d gave us to adhere to. Harboring the notion that after Sinai G-d changed or abandoned that code of law is no less absurd and dangerous than harboring the notion that since creation new laws of nature are in effect. Will a person who declares that the law of gravity 'has been fulfilled' and is, therefore, no longer in effect cause him to hit the pavement any slower were he to jump off a roof?

"So, too, is it dangerous for us to think that the laws of the Torah have been changed. Will we experience the negative fall-out of not fulfilling them any less because we espouse some theory that they are no longer in effect? It is our obligation to change ourselves to align with the Torah; it is not for us to say that G-d's Torah has been changed because it doesn't align with our impressions.

"Sinai has never been duplicated, and the Torah has never been changed. And that is why fulfilling and upholding the Torah is the message of Judaism and the mission of every Jew."

What is Life?

"I just can't believe that the answer to life is as simple as following the Torah."

"Let me ask you this then: What is the question to life?"

"The question?"

"Yes. How can you expect to understand the answer if you don't know the question?"

David paused. "You have a point, however, maybe there is no definitive question and, therefore, maybe life has no definitive answer."

"That is what society has taught you to believe."

"No. If anything, we are only taught to believe there are no absolutes."

"Are you *absolutely* sure about that?" the rabbi said with an exaggerated pause on the word 'absolutely.' "David, I meet with many young people — very intelligent and sophisticated young people — and my feeling is that a large percentage of them are confused because their absolute is that there are no absolutes.

You shouldn't be afraid to admit there is real meaning to life and that it is possible for you to know that meaning. Life is too short and filled with too many surprises to sit back and remain ambivalent."

"But," David replied, "I have also observed a lot of confused people who insist they have found the answer to life. It's very easy to fool yourself and say you have found the answer to life."

"Nevertheless, that does not preclude the possibility that there is a definite answer."

"True, however, I just don't see how the Torah is it."

"Why?"

"For one reason, because many of those rituals and laws don't seem to me to be relevant to life?"

"And what is life?"

"Life?"

"Yes. Life."

"Well . . . I don't really know."

"Then how can you say for sure that Torah is not addressing the very question of our purpose for living?" The rabbi paused. He then said, "David, I don't expect you to accept what I have to say right away. All I hope is that you are open to hearing it."

"Fair enough," David said. "What then is life? What is the real purpose of life? And I won't easily buy the claim that it is keeping the Torah — what is the purpose of keeping the Torah?"

"In order to answer you, I have to first explain to you

how the Torah views the world — the world that this life takes place on."

"Okay. I'll buy that."

Light and Shadow

"The first thing you have to understand, then," the rabbi said, "is that the world is not what it appears. Think of a computer. When you press the letter 'G' on the keyboard, are you really pressing the letter 'G'? No. You are pressing a representation of the letter 'G.' To the computer, the letter 'G' is nothing more than a series of electrical impulses. In fact, everything that you see on a computer screen or printout is nothing more than the result of some combination of 'electricity-on and electricity-off.'

"This world is real. Yet the reality is backed up by a more basic, idealistic form of the physical reality. Everything is in actuality some combination of light and shadow."

"What do you mean by that?"

"The Hebrew word for world is *Olam*. *Olam* also means concealed, hidden. The world, in essence, is a place where G-d conceals Himself. In other words, G-d partially covers up the projection of His own Self with an obstruction called *Olam*, the world.

"How do you show a movie? First, you have to have a projector strong enough to project light onto a screen. Second, you have to obstruct the light with a strip of film. In order to produce the images, you need darkened film. In fact, the better the film conceals the light, the nicer the image on the screen. When the light penetrates the film, an image comes out the other side onto a screen. Light projected through an obstruction becomes a man, a cat, a car. Thus, to show a movie, you need two things: a strong projector of light and a darkened strip of film which conceals the light.

"That is also the way G-d created the world. In the books of Jewish mysticism, G-d is called *ohr ain sof*, an infinite light. He can project himself to the farthest distances and the darkest depths. There is no place devoid of him, for if there was it would not exist (just as an image in a movie cannot be seen unless there is light to project it).

"How did G-d create the world? He obstructed the projection of His own Self with a filmstrip called *Olam*, the world. Just as each particular color and degree of shading on the filmstrip produces different shadows, everything in the world is another type of shadow. For instance, a tree is nothing but a concealment of the light that looks like a tree. We call it a tree, but in reality it is only another shadow of G-d. What is a cup of coffee? It is an obstruction of the infinite light. The concealment of light produces a shadow which we call a cup of coffee.

"Of course, unlike Twentieth Century Studios, G-d produces three-dimensional images which appear as material, tangible objects. Matter, though, is nothing more than a shadow. A shadow is a product of light.

"This world, then, is by definition the place where G-d hides Himself. It contains His light, i.e. the knowledge of Him, in a hidden way. And the purpose of life is to discover G-d; or as the prophet says: to fill the world with the knowledge of G-d."[3]

Why Does G-d Hide?

"If the goal is to find G-d," David asked, "why does He have to conceal Himself? Wouldn't it have been better for Him to make knowledge of Him easily available?"

"That is a good question. However, G-d concealed Himself in order to give us free will. For will to be free, the person must be placed between opposing choices. By concealing Himself, G-d gave man the option to see only the shadow or perceive the light behind the shadow."

"What's the big deal about free will? Why do we need it?"

"Because we come to value and enjoy discovering G-d only to the degree we overcome obstacles toward uncovering it. To draw an analogy: Welfare recipients tend not to feel good about the checks they receive because a hand-out does not taste the same as earned bread. Self-worth results only to the degree one works for his bread. So, too, with spiritual hand-outs — a human being feels good about it only to the degree he works for it.

"Therefore, it is in our own best interests to have free will in order to discover the light of G-d, even though that very same free will can be our downfall and lead us to choose the shadow. Free will is necessary because it gives us the opportunity to discover G-d of our own volition, to earn our knowledge of Him. If there were no challenge, we would not appreciate the discovery."

The Image in the Mirror

"If the world has so much of this potential for finding G-d, then maybe I should first travel around and see it before anything else. Then, one day, if I decide the Torah is for me, I will be all the better for it."

"You have to understand, David, that it is in the nature of a person to set out on a quest around the world only to find out in the end that all along the answer lay in his own heart. I'm sure you have read a lot of literature that explores that theme. It is very common.

"Why do people feel they have to travel the world in search of themselves?" the rabbi asked rhetorically. "Because, they fail to see the world inside of them. And just as the world is a combination of the light of G-d and an obstruction, so, too, is each person. In order to give man free will and the opportunity to earn his discovery of G-d, G-d gave man — into whom He projected Himself more than anything else — the darkest shadow. The dark shadow of man manifests itself in the ability to deny G-d.

"Of course, the absurdity of denying G-d is akin to the absurdity of a character in a film who gets up and denies he is part of the film. Nevertheless, G-d makes us so realistically that we can even deny the fact that we are shadows. He gave us so much of His light that in order to experience the challenge of uncovering it, He had to counteract it with the darkest of shadows.

"The challenge and test of life is to see beneath the thin veneer of 'reality' and recognize how we are shadows of G-d. Who are we? Who are those people projected on the movie screen? Nothing. As we say in the *Rosh Hashannah* prayers — 'Our days are like a passing shadow.'

"If what you are saying is true, rabbi," David asked, "then nothing matters anyway; we are nothing; our lives are worthless."

"No. As soon as we realize that we are shadows of the living G-d, the Essence of existence, we by force realize that our lives too have genuine existence. The knowledge that we are shadows should only produce humility. Humility is not feeling that you are worthless. Humility is the self-awareness to ascribe everything one does to G-d.

"Moses was the most humble of men.[4] He knew who he was. He knew G-d spoke to him like no one before or since.[5] Yet, he was the most humble of men. How? Because the more knowledge he acquired, the more he realized that he was nothing other than a shadow. As a shadow of G-d, he knew he couldn't take credit. His depth and clarity of vision did not let him take credit.

"Like a person standing next to the Empire State Building, whose feeling of humility results from awareness of the skyscraper, Moses's exceptional humility resulted from his exceptional awareness of G-d's greatness. That awareness led him to realize more genuinely than any other human being that his ability and successes were gifts from G-d. And that knowledge produced true humility, not denial over the worth of his actions.

"Therefore, to answer your question, David: Why is it beneficial to learn Torah first, before exploring the world? The answer is because we have a great potential to deny ourselves — to hide in our inner shadows and never step into the light. The world is beautiful, but it is only a mirror. In order to see ourselves in the world — as opposed to running away from ourselves into the world — we have to first know our selves; we have to be able to identify and recognize the part of our selves the world is meant to reflect. If you do not know how to identify that self, then you will not recognize it when you look in the mirror."

"What self are you talking about?"

"The Divine image in which G-d made us. This image, this true self, is hidden in the shadows of our heart. And, therefore, Torah is the place you should first search for yourself because it is the light and inner truth of the

Creator of the world. It is the closest reflection of His Self which can possibly exist. When you study and embody it, and when you can successfully identify your self with that Self reflected in the Torah, then when you look in the mirror — the world — the image reflected back at you will make sense."

The Buried Treasure and the Map

"When you say Torah, rabbi," David asked, "what exactly do you mean? Bible stories?"

"No. Torah is the inner truth of the Creator. The Creator expressed this inner truth in the form of Hebrew letters and words, which are referred to as the Five Books of Moses. These five books contain the way of life G-d designed for man, which would be reflective of that inner truth.

"And we do need the Torah because even though there is one G-d and many ways to serve Him, there are many more ways to mis-serve Him. Torah is not just a vaguely defined call to morality and spirituality. Many people want to be moral and spiritual, but their pursuit of these ideals is limited to what they can discern with their own finite, human understanding. And sooner or later the shortcomings of these idealistic-sounding yet mutable, man-made definitions of morality and spirituality become evident to all.

"Torah, on the other hand, is G-d's infinite understanding given to Moses on Mount Sinai in both the written form and the interpretation of the written form, the *Talmud* or oral Torah. Taken together, the Torah above all is the divinely-prescribed guidelines for living; it is a clearly defined lifestyle based on the 613 commandments. These commandments produce a very definite pattern of life. They are the skeletal structure around which the inner intent and soul of the Torah come to fruition."

"If the goal is knowledge of G-d why can't one just study it in a book?" David asked. "What does keeping all those commandments have to do with anything?"

"Because the highest knowledge is experiential knowledge. For instance, a child can be told that if he puts his hand in fire, he will get burned. However, when he actually puts his hand in the fire and gets burned he *knows* why he shouldn't put his hand in fire. Similarly, an artist can conceive of an idea but his whole art is his ability to make the idea more than an abstract notion.[6]

"G-d, spirituality, eternity, etc. are not solely for abstract thought, but are meant to be deeply perceived and experienced in a concrete, physical way. Therefore, G-d put us in the middle of an enormous, palpable world. We do not live only in a world of ideas. And, therefore, commandments which prescribe a lifestyle for living in the physical world are logical because they are the way of coming to know and reveal G-d in the world of action.

"Every aspect of our physical lives, including each

object of the physical world, is a potential treasure chest hiding within it some facet of the knowledge of G-d. Torah is the treasure map. Each commandment leads us to another buried treasure."

"Even the commandments which seem archaic and irrelevant?"

"They are only archaic and irrelevant to the superficial eye. Just as buried treasure is hidden in the most surprising places and one has to have the map and then dig beneath the surface to find the treasure, so, too, the buried treasure of the knowledge of G-d. It is in the world and the Torah lifestyle leads us directly to it."

Choose Life!

"Rabbi, even if I accept what you say I can't possibly see how living the 613 commandments is for me. I am used to freedom. How could I ever be happy giving it up?"

"The freedom you speak about is an illusion. Only when you keep the Torah can you actually be free."

"613 commandments sound to me like a lot of restrictions," David responded. "What type of freedom are you talking about?"

"Imagine a person was told he could go into the vault at Tiffany's and had one hour to grab all the gems he wanted. The hour begins, but since there is so much time, and he knows that he could grab more than he would ever need in half that time, he decides to let himself take in the sights for just a few moments.

"Mirrored displays, majestic fountains, gourmet food, amusements, interesting people, etc. — there are so many beautiful sights all around that he quickly loses himself in them. A half-hour goes by. Forty minutes. Fifty minutes. Fifty-five. Fifty-nine minutes go by, and all of a sudden he remembers: The hour, it's almost up! As the sixtieth minute strikes, he sees a gem lying around and grabs it.

"He leaves the store, goes to the jeweler next door, and asks how much it is worth. The jeweler looks at the stone and says excitedly, 'You want to sell this?'

"'Yes.'

"'I'll give you $100,000 dollars.' Now, David, let me ask you: How will this person react?"

"I would think he would be happy he came away with anything."

"You're right. At first he would be happy. However, afterwards the regret will sink in. 'Was I crazy?' he will tell himself over and over again. 'If in one moment I grabbed $100,000, in one hour I could have grabbed billions and billions of dollars worth of stones!'

"Our world," the rabbi continued. "is a Tiffany's. It possesses rare gems — elements of eternity — amidst a Disneyworld of temporary temptations and distractions, which although possessing their own momentary beauty only serve to draw one away from the real opportunity of grabbing diamonds, of grabbing our stake in eternity."

"What do you mean by eternity?"

"Eternity is the opposite of time. It is the experience where the barriers between creation and Creator are removed. And this is what the Torah tells us our choice is: time or eternity.

"This choice, in fact, is hinted in the first word of the Torah, *beraishis,* 'In the beginning.' *Beraishis* informs us that time itself was a creation. What existed 'before' the beginning? Only G-d. G-d is above time. He was, He is, He will always be. When He created the physical, material world, He created the framework of time.

"Creation — the physical world — is by definition the realm of the temporary. And therefore, our lives here consist of a limited number of moments; we exist in a prison made of time. On the other hand, however, there is an element of life which is above and beyond time — the eternity of G-d.

"An average person can live for as long as eighty or ninety years. If he lived for the sake of those eighty or ninety years — he lived time. If he came to the realization that this life cannot be an end in itself and he, in turn, chose to fulfill the purpose for which he was created he lived eternity — he made himself a partner with G-d in eternity.

"Creation is not an end in itself; it is a means. This life is a vehicle for us to transport ourselves from a framework of time into the experience of eternity, from the realm of the physical to the realm of the G-dly.

However, it is easy to get distracted and detoured; it is easy to become a prisoner of time.

"Freedom to walk into a prison is not freedom — it is an abuse of freedom. If we abuse our freedom and attach ourselves to things of an exclusively physical, temporary nature, we become chained to them — we lose the freedom to complete the very purpose for which we were placed here.

"Therefore, the restrictions of Torah are actually the mechanisms of freedom. They help us unshackle ourselves of time. They help us use our time to grab diamonds."

"I'm not sure I understand you."

"Let me illustrate it with our friend who was given the opportunity to enter the vault in Tiffany's. Imagine, beforehand, he was forewarned that he would be tempted with things which would distract him from grabbing the gems. To counteract the distractions, however, he was told that he would be given a list of 'do's and don'ts' which he was told he should follow, no matter what. These instructions would keep him focused on the task at hand and thereby insure that he would leave with enough wealth to buy his own Tiffany's.

"Beforehand, he may have dismissed the necessity of the instructions. Now in retrospect, after he blew his chance, he will appreciate the significance of the list of 'do's and don'ts.' They would have freed him from becoming entangled with the distractions. They would have freed him by telling him how to optimally use every moment of his precious time there. All he had to do was follow the instructions.

"That is the Torah. It helps us avoid getting hopelessly entangled in the temporary and steers us to the elements of eternity present in this temporary life. It is our list of instructions, telling us where we should go and where not to go, what we should do and what we shouldn't do, how we should do it and how we shouldn't do it. Every moment possesses the choice of time or eternity, and the Torah is our guide for choosing eternity."

"Can you give me an example?"

"Yes. Take eating, for instance. You can eat exclusively to fill your stomach, which is basically the same reason animals do, or you can turn your eating into a G-dly act by following the commandments the Creator gave you about eating. In the first case, you used your time to eat; in the second, you used it to gain eternity.

"Similarly, you can work, make a lot of money, and consider yourself self-made, or you can make your money and contemplate the help from Above, without which your seeming success would have never materialized.[7] In the former, your time is literally money — nothing less and nothing more; in the latter, your money brought you to a deeper appreciation of G-d and thereby helped you cash in time for eternity.

"Likewise, you can indulge in your natural urge for an intimate relationship and become more self-centered or you can marry, enjoy life with your spouse as the Torah prescribes, and change your orientation to one who is genuinely selfless.[8] In the former, your time of enjoyment lasted one night, one year, several years, but nothing more; in the latter, your time produced not only enjoyment but eternity.

"Eat, but know what to eat, how to eat, and why you are eating. Make a lot of money, but know how you are allowed to go about making money, what to do with it once you have it, and what is the true goal of making money. Marry and enjoy your relationship, but know the how, when, and why of your relationship. Every thing, every moment can be used — even the moments asleep in bed."

"How can you fulfill anything when you are asleep?"

"Sleep has a purpose: it keeps a person fresh and healthy. Since in order to serve G-d better and fulfill His Torah you need a healthy body, then your sleep can be a G-dly act, an act which converts time into eternity. Of course, you have to know how to go to bed, when to get up, and how to get up — and what to do with your health. However, when you do, even sleep is an opportunity to grab spiritual diamonds.

"That is what the Torah is all about. It is not an abstract philosophy or Bible stories. It is a way of life which seeks to help us convert the matter of the mundane elements from our everyday, worldly life into the spiritual energy of eternity. Each commandment, in its own way, teaches us how to make G-d a reality in our lives, to bring Him out from behind the murky shadows, and turn physical living into a tangible expression of spirituality.

"Food, money, time, relationships, human productivity and creativity — I have mentioned only a few examples. The list is as wide as the world. Life is beautiful, and even those things of temporary beauty can be used as tools to attain eternity. However, it is not possible to do so without the 'instructions for eternity' bequeathed to man by the Eternal G-d.

"'I put before you life and death, blessing and curse — choose life!'9 Notice, G-d doesn't exhort us, 'Don't choose death.' Why? Because remaining as we were born, just living our physical, finite existence without any boundaries or direction, leads to nowhere but death. And therefore death is not a choice; it is the natural outcome of our physical existence if we do not actively step forward and grab life.

"'Choosing life' means making the choice to faithfully follow the 'do's and don'ts' laid out in the Torah. By telling us specifically what to refrain from and what to partake of — and how to partake of it — the Torah teaches us how to really live. It is not a restriction. It is a life preserver. It helps us stay afloat and then teaches us how to swim beyond the horizon of our physical, time-bound lives."

CHAPTER 3

THE SECRET OF HAPPINESS

Happiness Versus Enjoyment

"Rabbi," David said, "the truth is that I can appreciate the value of living with limits, of being disciplined. If that is what the Torah does, then I understand a little better what you are talking about. However, the bottom line is that I am basically happy. I don't need religion."

"Are you really so happy?"

"Basically."

"Why do you qualify your happiness with the word basically?"

"I admit I have my moments of doubt. Life is not perfect. But basically I am reaching the point where this world is rewarding me for being a productive member. I can do a lot of the things I have always aspired to do. That doesn't mean that things always go my way."

"Based on what you just told me, let me rephrase my question: Are you happy or merely satisfied with the level of enjoyment you are presently receiving from the world?"

"I'm not sure I see the difference."

"There is a difference between happiness and enjoyment. Happiness is the result of pursuing a goal. Pursuit of the goal generates an energizing sense of purpose. Enjoyment, on the other hand, is an immediate sensation of pleasure; a person can enjoy a piece of cake, a piece of art, a good joke — it gives pleasure but then passes.

"Let me make this difference crystal clear to you with an illustration: Imagine you had a financial deal which could earn you ten million dollars literally overnight. All that it required was for you to personally show up in Sydney, Australia the next day to close the deal.

"You go to the airport, but they tell you all the tickets to the last flight have been sold, and the passengers are already boarding the plane. You can't hire a private plane, so you go to the airline manager, put down $20,000, and tell him to put you on the flight even if it means staying in the bathroom. He calls up the head steward, tells him the situation, and says, 'Listen, you take ten, and I'll take ten. Put him in the bathroom, and keep your mouth shut.'

"It is an excruciatingly long flight and you are chased out of the bathroom every ten minutes, but you are on the flight. On the same airplane is a man who inherited more money than he knows how to spend. His wife threw him out of the house, and he is miserable. Not knowing what to do with himself, he decided to take a flight in first class around the world. All the stewards and stewardesses jump at his beck and call because with every glass of champagne he leaves a $100 tip. He has money to burn and wants everyone to know it.

"Now, if one were to take a superficial look, who is the happiest passenger on that flight and who is the most unhappy? Anyone taking a quick look will say the passenger in first class with everyone ready to serve him is the happiest, and the one continually chased out of the bathroom and hounded is the most miserable.

"Of course, the truth is just the opposite. The happiest person on that flight is the man in the bathroom. The most miserable is the one in first class. What is the real difference? The passenger in the bathroom has a goal in taking the flight. As long as he has the goal clearly laid out in front of him, he is happy no matter which conditions he has to bear for the short term. The first class passenger, as long as he has no goal, is miserable no matter how pampered and provided for he is.

"We are on a plane, David. Our trip takes seventy or eighty years. If you want real happiness, find out your destination."

"But I'm not only living for moments of enjoyment," David assured the rabbi. "I have professional and personal goals."

"Those types of goals do not lead you to possess happiness. Take the typical medical student. What is the happiest moment of his life? His graduation. He worked and slaved for that moment. Once the moment passed, however, it was gone. He never really possessed happiness. It possessed him for a moment.

"I understand what you are saying," David said, "however, don't you agree that personal and professional goals are very important to a person's well being?"

"I admit they can help you get from point to point. However, even they can become pointless and circular if they do not lead to some ultimate point. So you become wealthy; what is the goal of having money? So you have 'made it' professionally; what do you do once you have finally 'made it'?

"Only a goal that transcends the self and reaches beyond this world can create a true state of happiness in a person. One can deceive himself to believe he is happy with smaller, finite goals, but at best that person is intoxicating himself with sporadic enjoyment."

Circular Reasoning

"But, rabbi," David asserted, "I'm not only interested in smaller, finite goals. I want the world to be safe from the threat of nuclear war; I want a clean environment; I want hunger eliminated. Those are larger goals."

"Those sound like noble goals, but, if you noticed, they are all related to the maintenance of the material world.

"What's wrong with that?"

"It is finite; it is circular," the rabbi said. "Think about it," he then suggested, "are you eating to live or living to eat?"

David thought for a moment. "Eating to live."

"Right. There is no real meaning in living to eat. However, why do most people work? To make money. Why do they need to make money? In order to eat. Why do they need to eat? In order to work. When you get down to it, they are living to eat."

"But people don't only make money in order to eat," David replied. He thought for a moment and then added, "I don't, at least."

"And what do you use your money for?"

"To make this world a little better place to live."

"And then we go back to the original question: What are you living for? What does it mean to live? What is life and its purpose?"

"Maybe it is simply to enjoy living."

"In other words," the rabbi said, "if 'eating' is symbolic of receiving enjoyment from the physical world, then in effect you are saying that you are living to eat." The rabbi waited a few moments for a response. Seeing none was coming he said, "People who make enjoying life their first commandment can never be happy because enjoyment is at best only a means. It tickles the senses for a period of time and then vanishes, leaving nothing but an insatiable desire for more. *When 'enjoying life' becomes the goal, it ceases producing happiness because the minute you get it you become dissatisfied.*

"Pursuit of a goal beyond tickling the self with enjoyment, on the other hand, by force produces happiness. When the goal takes up one's entire field of vision, then even the short-term withdrawal of enjoyment is in no way devastating."

"That makes sense," David admitted, "but I still don't understand how you can say that elimination of war, pollution and hunger are not real goals?"

"They may be larger than other goals," the rabbi responded, "but they do not get you out of the circle. In the final analysis, they are only goals to make this world run better. Let's say they would all come true; there would be no war, pollution or hunger. And then what?"

"Then everyone would be happy."

"Do you really think so? Would it really be any different than the passenger in first class? There would be no more goals. In fact, if that ever happened, the world would be more unhappy than ever."

"I find that hard to believe."

"Take a look around. See what has happened in this society. Has the wealth produced happiness? Or is all the talk about depression, suicide, rebellious children, greed, ingratitude and other problems as bad as, if not worse than, ever before?

"Just think about some of the terminology used in everyday language: for instance, the idea of 'killing time.' People feel they have to devise ways to kill time. They enslave themselves five days a week, fifty weeks a year, to be able to have the free time to watch television, read novels and take extravagant vacations. Vacation really means to vacate, to make time a void. People, nowadays, long for the time they can make their lives a void.

"This entire civilization's unique contribution to world history — the pyramids of the modern age — after all is said and done, I feel, is the entertainment business. Movies, television, sports, celebrities, videos, radios, commercials, docu-dramas, music and so on and so on — did you ever ask yourself what the reason is behind this entertainment explosion?

"Think about it. The booming entertainment industry is the symptom of a society dedicated toward tranquilizing its members with a lifetime of enjoyments. The symptoms tell you that the patient is ill with the disease of lacking real goals. The participants of this society do not know what life is, and therefore have to create something to block out reality, to fill the time, to vacate their minds, to escape into a void. If they ever attained the goal of world peace and had to face the void 52-weeks a year they'd really go crazy.

"However, life is not a void. For over 3,300 years the

Jewish people have been trying to tell the world that; we have been fighting to maintain our focus on the real purpose of life, in the face of civilizations who worshipped idols, produced inquisitions, pogroms, holocausts, and now promote or cultivate atheism, pseudo-religion, cultism and the god of entertainment."

"You make it sound as if there is no idealism outside of your circle. There is a lot of idealism out there."

"I am willing to admit, David, that the world is not lacking idealistic people. But, when it comes down to it, what are the *world's* ideals? Where is most of the idealistic energy of its people funneled into?

"At the turn of this century, the world was filled with so much optimism for the future that people were sure we were on the verge of a new age, a brave new world. Jewish people in particular exchanged their time-proven values for the new idealism like that of the communists or the Germans with their high culture. Looking back now at the end of this century, did their idealism get them anywhere? Or did their allegiance to the ideals of the outside world perpetuate their own destruction?

"Take an honest look at the world. I think an objective person has to conclude that this last century has been the most murderous and inhumane in world history, not only for the Jewish people but in general. Upon close inspection, it is as if the more mankind has 'advanced,' the further away from a perfected world it has drifted."

"How could that be?"

"Because it does not have a real ideal. Ideals like ecology, technology, culturalism, communism, capitalism, etcetera are, at best, means to an end. Their focus is ultimately some form of material comfort.[10] And when you turn what is in reality a material means into an end, and pursue it, you forget about or move further from the true end.

"You were right, David: The world is not lacking idealistic people, but it doesn't know how to harness or where to steer its idealistic yearnings because the real end goal of life is still a mystery to it. And as long as it lacks a real ideal, even its idealistic individuals are impotent to affect, or can become impediments to attaining, the ultimate goal.

"We all have to ask ourselves the following question," the rabbi concluded: "What is the purpose of this world? If the material world has no higher purpose other than perpetuating itself, then, we are only living to eat; the best we can hope for is circling the globe in the vacuum of a first class 365-day-a-year paid vacation. On the other hand, if our material existence is a means to a higher purpose — and elimination of war, hunger and pollution enhance material existence — then peace, cooperation and plenty first acquire value because they become part of the means to that higher purpose."

The Ultimate Purpose

David paused and remained quiet in thought for a few moments. "But what can be higher than world wide peace, cooperation and plenty?"

"To simplify it, the highest ideal one can ever aspire to is to serve G-d."

"Serve G-d?"

"Yes."

"G-d needs us to serve Him?"

"No. We need to serve G-d. Every human being has a primal need to serve G-d."

"Every human being? Even ones who don't believe in G-d?"

"Yes. If they don't identify that need with G-d, they identify it with something less exalted. Nevertheless, all of us, in some way, have to cast our energies and allegiances toward something higher than ourselves. Even those who don't think they do. Take the phenomenon of sports, for instance.

"Every team has a following of millions of fans. Most of these fans spend exorbitant amounts of money on buying tickets, paraphernalia and other related items; to find out how their team is doing, they devote huge chunks of time watching television, reading newspapers, listening to the radio, and having discussions with friends; they indoctrinate their children to their favorite teams at an early age; they get frustrated when their team is frustrated and exuberant when their team excels; they live and die with the team, whose own fate is often decided with an incalculable bounce of a ball; they shout 'We're number one' as if they themselves were a paid performer on the team.

"Idealists and materialists; intellects and simpletons; those involved in cultural movements or counter-cultural movements; societies pushing fads in dress, music, soft drinks; people affiliating with political parties, corporations, careers, and so on and so on — everyone has a tremendous need to serve or identify with something larger than himself or herself.

"The question is not: Do we identify with something or not? The question is: What do we identify with?

"The ultimate identification is with G-d. And that is why serving Him is the ultimate fulfillment."

"I can agree with you, then, that there is an important human need to serve or identify with something larger than ourselves," David said. "However, there are a lot of things larger than ourselves that are not G-d — and not just superficial things like baseball teams or fads."

"Man-made identities and philosophies — no matter what they are — are limited because, by definition, they are made by man, who is limited. Ultimately, the best a man can do is define his own idealism and sacrifice himself for it. In reality, self-defined idealism is not really idealism. It is ultimately only serving the self, a self which one projects onto the ideal he or people similar to him made up."

"For instance, we always hear of people whose express goal is to serve humanity. Then, when you examine the private lives of many of these self-styled idealists, you often find that they were not faithful to their spouses or they, in some way, neglected or abused their closest circle of friends and family. People like that use serving humanity as a smoke screen for serving themselves. They may even fool themselves with the smoke screen, but they can't hide behind it forever. Sooner or later, the truth comes to the surface that, all along, they were really only serving themselves."

"What is really so bad about serving yourself?"

"For one thing, deep down each of us realizes that if there is nothing more than the four corners of our own selves, then life is not very meaningful. Yes, there can be moments of enjoyment and pleasure. However, in the end, a person cannot feel meaning in his life if all he does is serve himself."

"I don't agree. A person has to look out for himself."

"I am not saying that self-interest is inherently bad," the rabbi responded. "The great Torah sage Hillel said,[11] 'If I am not for myself, who will be?' We have to be out for ourselves. However, Hillel continues, 'Yet, living for myself, what does that make me?' In other words, a person who lives only for himself is not much of a human being. Therefore, while it is true that we first have to have a self — because without that self we have nothing to serve G-d with — if somewhere down the line we do not turn our vision outside of ourselves, then our lives become meaningless."

"According to what you are saying," David said, "if a person doesn't believe in G-d, then there is no way he can be doing anything other than serving himself."

"Exactly."

"I can't agree with that."

"If not G-d, then tell me whom they are serving?"

"Well . . . I don't know, but, for instance, I have a friend who is a psychiatrist, and he doesn't believe in G-d, yet he tells me he gets great pleasure in helping others."

"I don't know him personally, but next time you see him ask him if he would be as selfless in his helping others if his position didn't afford him a high salary and status in society. If there is no G-d, then all that remains is self-interest. Without the ultimate goal of serving G-d, then even helping others, as noble as it sounds, is either the naive ideal of a fool or nothing more than a guise for helping oneself."

Disciples to the Master Artist

David sat paused in thought for a moment. The rabbi could see on his face that he was not satisfied. "Maybe I just don't easily relate to the idea of serving G-d," David finally said. "Maybe you will think that I am self-centered and egotistical for asking this, but what do I really gain by serving G-d? What is in it for me? I hope you don't throw me out for saying that, but that is the way I feel."

"I appreciate your honesty. Many who don't have the courage to ask that question, think it nonetheless."

"Is there really an answer?"

"Yes. Serving G-d is the way to gain knowledge of Him. What's so great about that?" the rabbi asked rhetorically. "What's in it for us? you ask. That is its own reward. In fact, that is the ultimate reward. G-d is the source of life, knowledge — everything — and gaining a close, intimate knowledge of G-d through our service to Him is the ultimate experience. He is the ultimate mystery — and thus the ultimate discovery."

"If that is so, then once we know Him there is nothing more to live for."

"No. G-d is infinite; there is no end to knowing Him. Just look at the physical world He created: you can explore outward into the 'infinite' expanse of space, or inward into the equally 'infinite' expanse of the atom. And if this world, no matter how infinite it seems, is only a finite creation, then the true infinity of its Creator is beyond description."

"If He is so infinite, then how can we ever know Him at all?"

"G-d's essence is unknowable, however, the creation He put us in and made us part of is our vehicle for attaining an otherwise unattainable knowledge of Him."

"If that's the case," David asked, "then you should be

a scientist studying nature, not a rabbi who studies holy books."

"No. If nature is the Artist's painting, then Torah is the ways and wisdom of the Artist Himself. Studying nature is like studying the Artist's painting. Studying Torah is like living as an apprentice to or disciple of the Artist. Just as an apprentice artisan serves the master artisan in order to learn his ways and wisdom, so, too, do we learn to emulate G-d by serving Him through performing His Torah. Torah reveals to us the attitude and behaviors reflective of G-d's essence which He wants us to emulate."

"What type of behavior and attitudes does G-d have?"

"In essence, He is beyond behavior and attitudes. Nevertheless, He clothes Himself, so to speak, with certain human attributes which He knows are beneficial for us. For instance, He is merciful and expects us to, likewise, be merciful; He epitomizes wisdom and, so, too, are we encouraged to pursue wisdom. When we embrace the G-dly attributes, we gain a closeness to G-d which the study of G-d's creation alone cannot produce.

"No one understands one artist like another artist, and only through living the Torah can one come to an insider's knowledge of the Creator. By studying it and following its instructions for living we, in our own way, turn ourselves into creative artists similar to Him.[12] That is the greatest personal and universal ideal anyone can possess."

Mysticism in Everyday Life

"Rabbi," David said, "I have to admit that I like a lot of what you are saying. It is not so unbelievable to me that there is a G-d and that knowing Him is the ultimate experience. And the way you explained it, I can understand how serving Him is the way to know Him.

"Furthermore, I must have had some interest in these ideas even before I came here, otherwise I would never have attended your lecture or decided to speak to you. The truth is that I never was and still am not completely closed to the idea of learning more about Judaism and even attending synagogue a little. Nevertheless, most of life is not attending synagogue or performing rituals. Most of life is working for a living and having to solve problems of a non-religious nature. And, therefore, as nice as some of the things you are saying sound, religion seems irrelevant to me. Practically speaking, what do these high ideas have to do with a person's everyday, secular activities?"

"The truth of the matter," the rabbi answered, "is that there is no such division as you just expressed. A Jew should not view life as a separate sphere for religious functions and a separate sphere for secular, non-religious functions. We do one thing: We serve G-d. Serving G-d manifests itself in different ways. Sometimes we pray, sometimes we do business, sometimes we sit and learn. In fact, since it is all one thing anyway, it is possible to flip-flop everything around, and perform one activity while immersed in another."

"What do you mean by that?"

"Take a businessman, for instance. While praying, he is doing business, and while doing business, he is praying."

David tried to decipher the rabbi's words, but could not. After a few seconds, he looked at the rabbi and said, "I don't understand."

"Since," the rabbi began to answer, "G-d created a world where eating is a means to the task of living — as we said, man eats to live, not lives to eat — He made our eating dependent on Him so that we can make our main focus the business of living.[13] Even though He expects each of us, in varying degrees, to bring home an income in a natural way,[14] He is in ultimate control of our standard of living. Now, if that is so — if our eating is in actuality dependent upon Him — then when are we really making a living?

"The answer is: In prayer. A Torah businessman says his morning prayers in the following way: 'G-d, You gave me life; I am sure that it is You who also provide for the daily substance which sustains my life. Nevertheless, I have to go out in order to bring home that sustenance; You want me to work for a living. You also want me to turn to You in my prayers to seek Your help. I need Your help. I know my own efforts alone will get me nowhere. I am asking You now, therefore, to please give me my sustenance to the maximum, in the easiest way —

without challenges and worries.'

"Therefore," the rabbi said, "when is this Jew doing his best business? Not at the negotiating table, but before ever getting to the office, while he is praying to G-d. That is when he is really earning his income. That is doing business while he prays.

"Next," the rabbi continued, "he comes to the office and gets a phone call. It is a prospective customer. Immediately he turns to G-d and prays: 'G-d, please let him accept my terms.' Similarly, every contact in his day is like this: 'G-d, please don't let me be fooled . . . please have the bank give me the loan . . . please don't let them charge me too much' — everything he feels a real need for, he prays to G-d for. In effect, then, when is he praying his best? In the office."

"But isn't that using G-d for the wrong reasons?"

"It ultimately depends on the underlying attitude. If a person truly views making money as a means of deepening his prayers to G-d (and not the reverse, where making money is his real goal and he happens to turn to G-d because he thinks G-d can help him make more), then he is serving G-d (as opposed to serving himself) even through his business endeavors. After all, G-d is G-d in the synagogue or the office. As long as you use both situations to turn to Him and deepen your relationship with him, then you are living a truly Jewish life."

"That is very profound," David said. "In effect, you are

saying that there really is no such thing as the mundane."

"Exactly. There is unfathomable mysticism in everyday life. Everyday life, which includes the so-called religious and mundane, contains the hidden knowledge of G-d, and the 613 commandments of the Torah are the clues to uncovering another facet of that knowledge. Torah is the guide which helps us make our entire life one long, continuous chain of gaining knowledge of and serving G-d."

"I think I finally understand you," David said. "It's funny, I always thought of Judaism as a bundle of commandments, some of which are relevant and some not. However, you are saying that it really encompasses everything."

"That's what I've been trying to tell you."

David thought for a moment and then asked, "But do the 613 commandments really include everything?"

"The truth is that even taking into account all 613 commandments, there is room for a great amount of neutral activities. However, there is an entire field of Torah called the duties of the heart, which encompass the inner person — his thoughts, aspirations and underlying motives. When one has his duties of the heart in mind, then no activity is neutral.

"The 613 commandments are the bare minimum requirements. I would venture to say they don't take up more than twenty to thirty percent of life. They certainly leave a great deal of room for a neutral area. However, the opportunistic individual who wants to perfect his inner self — and all of us should strive to be opportunistic — seeks to turn everything into a *mitzvah*. To him, there is no such thing as neutral ground. That, by the way, is the idea of *Chassidus*."

"*Chassidus*?" David asked.

"Yes. *Chassidus* really means doing more than is required by the letter of the law."

"I thought it was a sect of religious Jews."

"The Chassidic Movement, started 250 years ago, only sought to reemphasize ideas like that. The idea of a *chassid*, though, is something which has always existed in Torah life. It means going beyond the letter of the law. It doesn't mean changing the law, like adding a six-hundred-fourteenth commandment. It means doing more with the 613; it means turning the neutral ground of Torah law into a service to G-d.

"'In all your ways know Him.'[15] Every moment of our everyday existence can be used to achieve the ultimate purpose — bringing the knowledge of G-d into our lives. That is the way we serve G-d. The goal is to turn everything into one long chain of serving G-d."

The Key to Happiness

David got up out of his seat and walked around. He gazed out of the window a moment, turned to the rabbi and said, "Rabbi you are beginning to make sense — and that scares me. I'm not saying I'm convinced, but for the first time in my life, I understand how an intelligent person can maybe take this stuff seriously.

"However," he continued, sitting back in his seat, "I don't want to get carried away. I want to know one thing: Are people really happy in your community?"

"The happiest and most fulfilled people are in our community. Of course, no one is perfect, and, to varying degrees, all of us fall short of our ideals. However, the more deeply one embraces the Torah outlook, the more truly happy he is."

"How can you say that so confidently?"

"Because a Jew who knows what being a Jew is all about is never unhappy since he knows that no situation in life prevents him from fulfilling his purpose in creation — from serving G-d. Whether immersed in the 'mundane' or 'spiritual,' any Jew can thrive and feel great accomplishment. And that knowledge — the knowledge that you are in pursuit of a goal, the highest possible goal, the goal of serving G-d — is the key to happiness. In fact, that knowledge is so powerful for personal happiness that it can turn even failure into a fulfilling experience."

"How?"

"Because the truth is that we are not truly in control of our lives anyway. I lecture a lot to childless couples, who particularly need to understand this point. G-d commands us to have children, I tell them. Now, why does He have to make it a commandment; isn't it greater for people to want to have children voluntarily of their own volition?

"However, every commandment is a divine mission. As a divine mission, every step preparatory to the fulfillment of that mission becomes a fulfillment of G-d's will. In other words, the end result is not the only criterion for success. And, therefore, a divine commandment transforms every means to the end result into a goal itself.

"For instance, if everything is well, a pregnant woman goes through nine months of morning sickness, discomfort, and mood swings which finally culminate in excruciating labor pains. Despite all the discomfort, in the end she looks at the newborn and says it was all worth it.

"Now, what if she was pregnant for a few months and then, G-d forbid, miscarried? How devastating! She will tend to think that all the suffering and effort were for nothing.

"However, when she can say to herself: 'G-d commanded me to have children; it is my business to try and fulfill that commandment, however, I have no guarantee about the end result. I know that as long as I am taking all the necessary steps to fulfill this mission, then I am a success — mission accomplished.' When she can say that and mean it, then she is never devastated. In fact, in a sense, every second she is pregnant she is giving birth to a child. Her feeling of accomplishment is not dependent on the final outcome, which is really only in G-d's hand anyway.

"We are like data processors," the rabbi continued. "A data processor doesn't see the final printout while punching the keys. All he knows is that the instructions call for him to enter such and such information at such and such a point, and press such and such a button when he is prompted. The computer, in turn, will process all the information and in the end give a printout.

"The Torah is G-d's instruction book to us detailing how to serve Him. As long as I follow the instruction manual and screen prompts, I can feel assured that I am positively contributing to the printout — I know I am serving G-d. That fulfills me and serves G-d all at the same time."

"I will give you one more example; this one from my personal life. Just two weeks ago, I was on my way to give a seminar in Atlanta, Georgia. My flight was scheduled to depart at 12:30, but was delayed three hours. The terminal was stuffy and congested with people.

"I sat down and thought to myself as follows: 'G-d, You had given me a mission to teach Torah — the greatest of the 613 commandments — to people in Atlanta. If my mission is to get to Atlanta, Georgia to give a seminar, then this time is wasted, and my mission is a failure. However, my real mission is to perform Your will, to serve You. You have merely given me a different mission, namely, the mission to be stuck in a hot, stuffy airport for a few hours. Since You are in my life even now, then every moment is a potential goal in itself. Therefore, I will sit here, serve You, and turn this into a productive situation.'"

"But what did you really gain by sitting there?" David asked.

"I'll mention a few things just off the top of my head: One, I was able to remind myself once more that my purpose in life is to serve G-d. And when things don't always go my way, I am happy because I can always serve G-d. In fact, when they don't go my way, I am even more happy because it is a greater challenge to successfully serve G-d in that situation.

"Next, who knows how many people were positively effected when they saw an observant Jew sitting there calm, relaxed, happy, learning Torah and saying afternoon prayers while everyone else was pacing about, hot and aggravated?

"Last, in the end I still made it to Atlanta in time and related this incident over at the Seminar. One boy came up to me afterwards and told me he was so satisfied with this particular story, that it helped him to finally decide to go learn Torah. If my goal was not to serve G-d but subtly to serve myself through the honor of giving a lecture to a large audience in Atlanta then I would have been distraught over the delay and would have probably lost all these gains.

"The truth, David, is that I don't have to know what I gain; in fact, if I gain absolutely nothing else, whenever I uphold the Torah ideal to the best of my ability I know that I have served G-d. And that knowledge is the fuel of happiness. It is not always in our hands to do everything. The only thing that is necessary for happiness is to know what the Torah tells you to do at the moment and try your best to do it.

"David, the tree of life in the midst of the surging waters — that Torah attitude of mind — is the right of every Jew. The only price you have to pay to attain it is a commitment of time — honest time. Torah is not just a philosophy; it is a way of life. Go and learn; see how true it is, and then analyze how to deal with the other variables in your life."

CHAPTER 4

LEARNING AND RETURNING

That was the "The Conversation" — at least the way David remembered it. He told it to Cindy, his girlfriend, who, somewhat to his surprise, was even more interested in what the rabbi had to say than he.

"Very often," David remembered the rabbi saying at that first lecture, "you find a couple intermarried or considering intermarriage, where the non-Jewish partner is more interested in Judaism than the Jewish one! The reason is because to the non-Jew, keeping the Torah is not a threat. They are not afraid to ask questions because, deep down, they know it does not obligate them to change. A Jew, though, deep down knows the implications of finding out that the Torah is true, and is afraid to get anywhere near the subject. Therefore, it is not uncommon to hear of a conversation involving an intermarried or intermarrying couple where the non-Jew asks all the questions, while the Jewish partner sits there aloof and scoffs."

David was not a scoffer, however, it did surprise him how interested Cindy was. After thinking it over, she even encouraged him to take time off — and fly to Jerusalem, if need be — to study!

In actuality, David wrestled with the possibility of studying at all for some time. He had one more particularly crucial conversation with the rabbi about his fear of being brainwashed.

"Brainwashing," the rabbi told him, "is accomplished through tactics like depriving the newcomer of sleep, inundating him with information which he is not encouraged or allowed to respond to, and never letting him think for himself. A *yeshiva* is just the opposite. More or less, you choose which classes to attend. And, not only are you allowed and even encouraged to respond to whatever you are taught, you are not succeeding at Torah learning until you learn to question and challenge. Learning Torah entails constant questioning, dialogue,[16] reflection and thinking for oneself. The more one does so, the more the *yeshiva* has reached its goals."

In the end, David started attending night classes at a local *yeshiva* recommended to him by the rabbi. He found other people from all types of backgrounds converging on the school for reasons similar to his own. 'Why? Why? Why?' 'Who are you?' and 'What is this Judaism business really all about?' motivated most of the peers he met. Slowly, he began to open up to the whole experience. He found himself growing in ways he never thought he would. Gradually, he developed an ever-deepening thirst for the words of Torah.

During the first weeks of his initiation into Torah learning, he never broke his relationship with Cindy. In fact, she was still very interested in what he was learning and what new discoveries he had made. She herself was reading what she could about the Torah. However, they did not talk about the implications to their relationship. Nevertheless, they both sensed that the day would come when they would have to confront it.

Well, the day came.

David woke up and found his thoughts tearing at his insides. He could not push it off any longer. Forgoing his other responsibilities, he found a quiet place at home to reflect on his situation and sort out his emotions. Groping for some guidance, that is when he found his old diary and began reading it.

Why? Why? Why? Why did it have to be so hard? There had been a lot of loneliness before she came into his life. He was grateful to her for relieving him of that. He was more than grateful. He still loved her. What could he do, though? How could he live with the inconsistency?

These were the thoughts going through his mind when the phone rang. It was Cindy. She sounded excited. Her excitement, though, only saddened David because he was seriously wrestling with the possibility of breaking up the relationship at that moment.

"I'm glad you called," he said, "because I've been doing a lot of thinking."

"David, I've been doing a lot of thinking, too," she interrupted excitedly, "and before you say what you have to say, I want to tell you that I have come to a major conclusion in my life. It's something that will solve all our problems. What I've decided, basically, is that . . ."

CHAPTER 5

WHO IS A JEW?

"Let me get this straight," the rabbi said to David and Cindy as they sat in his office, "she is going to keep the 613 commandments in all their detail — keeping strictly *kosher,* observing *Shabbos,* etcetera — yet remain a non-Jew?"

"Yes. It seems to satisfy both our needs," David replied. "She has been reading a lot of Torah books and is as interested in it as I am. To convert is a big thing, but she's intrigued with the lifestyle enough to really take it up. And I believe she means it sincerely."

"I'm not doubting her sincerity, but the Torah is quite explicit that a Jew is forbidden to marry a non-Jew under any circumstances. There is no way of getting around it."

"But why? Isn't it more important who a person is

than what religion he or she happened to be born into?"

"David, everything that happens is carefully designed by G-d. There is no such thing as coincidence. And, therefore, you can be sure that being born Jewish is not incidental to who you are, just as being born non-Jewish is not incidental to who she is."

"I don't have anything against being Jewish," David replied. "In fact, I appreciate it more now than ever before. However, if another human being is a good person, then what does it matter whether the person is Jewish or not? If you were to ask me which I am first: a Jew or a human being? I would answer: a human being."

"You only say that because you don't really know what a Jew is."

"Perhaps. However, I know what a human being is."

"And what is your definition of a human being?"

"Someone who is a good person."

"Everyone thinks he is a good person. Hitler thought he was a good person. In his mind, the Aryans were not just human beings but super human beings. Therefore, wiping out Jews and other peoples was advancing the cause of humanity. That was his definition of good. And if you grew up a non-Jew in Nazi Germany, you would have had the same definition of good. In whatever society you are raised and in whatever situation you are raised, you will tend to think that you are good and in the right, no matter how bad and wrong you may be."

"I would add to that definition, then," David said,"

that a human being is a person who doesn't hurt others."

"Imagine it was 1933 and you had the opportunity to kill Hitler: Would you do it?"

"Well . . . maybe . . . probably."

"I would hope so because if you didn't, it would be one of the most inhumane acts imaginable. By killing him in 1933, you would have saved millions and millions of lives."

"Well, then, maybe there are certain times and instances when it is necessary to cause the downfall of evil like Hitler."

"When are those times, and what is evil, and who determines that?"

"I guess one has to have given these questions a lot of thought."

"Whose thought? Subjective human thought? The thought of philosophers like those who had such a profound impact on Nazi philosophy? David, I think that when you reflect on it a little, you will see how futile it is to live with a man-made definition of good, with a man-made definition of what constitutes a human being. If there is such a definition, it has to come from a source which is above and beyond the human perspective."

"I can see the need for that."

"Then without even claiming to possess that definition, how can you say you are a human being? What is a human being? What is a Jew? What do you mean that you are a human being before a Jew?"

"You have a good point, rabbi," David admitted. "I guess what I meant is that a human being is a term for the common society of mankind. And being Jewish, after all, is basically an ethnic orientation, one of many ethnic orientations within this common society. Would you agree with me about that?"

"No."

"Why not?"

"Because a Jew is not an ethnic or national entity."

"What do you mean?"

"The beginning of the Jewish people is different from all other peoples' beginning. Others formed themselves to fulfill their own needs. We were formed to fulfill G-d's needs."

"I'm not sure I understand."

"People in Italy, for instance, decided to get together in order to put up a government which would serve them — to build roads, set up an army, acquire wealth, etcetera. They also had common foods, mannerisms, language, identifying with each other through their common ethnic interests. The result today is that there exists an ethnic group called Italians.

"The Jewish people, on the other hand, did not form themselves. G-d forged us into a people in the iron furnace of the Egyptian exile, took us out of bondage, led us to Mount Sinai, and charged us forever to keep His Torah. Only afterward did a homeland, and the trappings that go with it, come.

"Thus, our common identity is not in essence ethnic or even national. Jews in Yemen and Sephardic lands do not identify with gefilte fish and the combination of German and Hebrew referred to as Yiddish. Yet, despite almost 2,000 years of lacking nationhood and in the absence of ethnic commonality, the Jew in Yemen and the Jew in New York are equally Jewish."

"What is the common bond, then?"

"One thing: G-d created us to serve Him. Anything else which people commonly identify as Jewish is superficial and ultimately non-essential. Only identification with the mission of Israel, which is to serve G-d, and the Torah, which is the explanation of how to serve G-d, are essential to Jewish identity.

"Being Jewish, therefore, is more than being merely a human being. G-d made man in His image but until Sinai humanity had no definite obligation to serve G-d, to bring to fruition the majesty inherent in that image. Nothing really stopped a person from using the image of G-d in the service of himself.

"A Jew, on the other hand, is a human being who is descended from Abraham, Isaac, and Jacob, the forefathers whom G-d said distinguished themselves in their service to Him. The book of *Beraishis* (Genesis) is singly devoted to that fact. And first it emphasizes their distinguishing characteristics as individuals, then as a family, and finally as a nation. G-d led this nation to Sinai and made them distinct, establishing forever an irrevocable special relationship with everyone born from their offspring."

"Wait. Are you saying that a Jew is more than a human being merely because he has a genetic link extending back a few thousand years? And, if so, isn't that similar to the type of prejudice you just told me Hitler had?"

"No. First, as a creation made in the image of G-d, all human beings, at the minimum, deserve great respect; they are certainly not to be considered vermin. Second, there is no prejudice because any non-Jew can become a Jew. By contrast, in the Nazi conception of being an Aryan, you were either born Aryan or not. It was based on ethnic, racial considerations which were solely determined by birth.

"Furthermore, the Torah definition of a human being fulfilling G-d's highest ideal, i.e. a Jew, is very different even from other religions. Other religions are exclusive: you have to be one of them, or not only do you lose heaven but you live forever in hell. In the Christian or Moslem scheme of things, there is no room for non-Christians or non-Moslems.

"Judaism is inclusive. It has always maintained that not only is it possible for individuals outside the religion to be righteous (as non-members), but they can even earn an other-worldly reward for their righteousness. It is truly universal and encompasses all of mankind because the bottom line is that everything depends on the individual's righteousness, the individual's fulfillment of G-d's will.

"Not including cultures and religions which sanction things like idolatry, murder, immorality, theft and the like, the Torah recognizes there are many ways to be righteous. Non-Jews can elect to pursue righteousness as they are, or go beyond that and join us in taking up the unique mission G-d chose to give us. In either case, there is no prejudice because they are not limited by birth or to a narrow, exclusive belief."

The Need for a Chosen People

"Why does one have to become a Jew first? Why can't a non-Jew try to live up to this higher calling without identifying with the Jewish people? I guess what I am asking is: why was there any need for G-d to choose one people over another? I still have trouble with the whole notion that the Jewish people are the chosen people."

"Let me briefly explain it to you from the beginning, then," the rabbi said. "G-d had a purpose when He created the world. If Adam had fulfilled G-d's will, the world would have reached the eternal, perfected state G-d created it for. Adam failed, and a mankind increasingly alienated from its Maker proliferated.

"Nine generations passed, and then Noah gained the focus of the Torah's attention. He was righteous, but in the end he did not fully actualize G-d's purpose for creation.[17] So, G-d waited.[18] He waited, and then Abraham stepped forward. In a spiritual vacuum,

Abraham rediscovered the Creator and what it meant to be His creation.

"Not surprisingly, then, with the introduction of Abraham, everything else in G-d's view falls to the background. Monumental history is happening all about, yet the Author of the Torah found it more important to detail the life and struggles of this one individual, Abraham. Why? Because through him, G-d now had a way of reforging all of civilization in the mold of righteousness. Abraham's private thoughts and actions would prove to mean more, in the long run, than the building of towers, pyramids and all the other otherwise momentous events going on at his time.

"Abraham was the beginning of the Jewish people, the first of three forefathers chosen by G-d to be the cornerstone of G-d's design to rebuild all of mankind. True, if Adam had been worthy there would have been no need for a chosen people. All mankind would have in essence been chosen.[19] However, early mankind deviated from the purpose of creation. Therefore, when the forefathers made themselves worthy, G-d chose them to commence the long, evolutionary process of restoring the world to its original grandeur.

"Thus, it is not far-fetched to say that the Jewish people are the chosen people. G-d chose us for the mission of bringing the original, universal theme of creation to all of mankind."

Israel

"What exactly is the mission you refer to?"

"The same mission Abraham pursued: bringing mankind to a true recognition of G-d."

"But even according to what you are saying, rabbi," David replied, "most of the world recognizes G-d. Most of it is no longer primitive or superstitious. Maybe they don't all share Judaism's understanding of G-d, but in essence Abraham succeeded. Maybe the Jewish mission is complete?"

"No."

"Why?"

"Because although the general world does not mind admitting there is a G-d, its understanding of G-d is laced with alien, self-designed fabrications. These distortions frustrate the plan of creation and will need to be clarified before the world reaches its ultimate destiny."

"Specifically, what distortions are you talking about?"

"Basically two: the misconceptions concerning Torah and Israel. Torah is the definitions of life, humanity, goodness, etc. from the Divine perspective, which human beings must have if they hope to move beyond subjective, man-designed ideals. Israel is the human stock fashioned by G-d and charged with the responsibility to fulfill the Torah. Until the world understands that the true conception of G-d and His intent is fulfilled through the dual blossoming of Torah and Israel, mankind's conception of G-d is not complete."

"But, rabbi, you yourself told me that the Christians and Moslems concur that the giving of the Torah at Mount Sinai happened; and many of them even agree that G-d chose the Jewish people to keep the Torah."

"True. Yet, in effect, they deny it because they consider the Torah an 'Old' Testament, not applicable any longer. They claim things like: G-d abolished the obligation to observe the Torah because He saw it was too hard for human beings. In saying things like that they completely overlook statements in the Torah like: "The commandments I command you today are not too difficult for you or distant . . . rather the matter is very near to you, already in your mouth and in your heart, in order to do."[20]

"There is no end to their claims. Our job, though, is not to engage them in debate but to tell the world there is a Torah — not through force or domination, but through modeling the blinding light of its truth. That is the way Abraham did it. As his descendants, we have a mission to observe the Torah's laws and saturate ourselves with its spirit not only for our own sakes, but, in addition to give sincere onlookers the opportunity to see the truth and beauty of the Torah's ways.

"That is the Jewish mission. And clearly, our mission is not over. We are still very much in the process of completing it. This mission has never been taken away, superseded, replaced or in any way changed for over

3,300 years."

"I can understand the idea of Torah," David said. "You have explained that to me well in the past: G-d gave mankind teachings in order to help us make the most out of life. And learning the Torah these past few weeks I am beginning to see the depth of its logic, and the truth of its ways. However, while the Torah may be true and perfect, Jews are by no means perfect."

"True. Ignorance of the Torah plus sin, compounded by persecution, have taken their toll on us. Nevertheless, no matter how far we stray, as descendants of the righteous forefathers, G-d waits for us — only us — to embrace His Torah and bring the purpose of creation to full fruition."

"But why?"

"Because just as the Torah was in G-d's plans before He created the world, so, too, Israel was in G-d's plans before He created the world.[21] In other words, the creation of the world was only to serve as a stage for the twin concepts of Torah and Israel."[22]

"Stop here," David said. "The world was created for the sake of Torah and Israel?"

"Yes. Torah, as I told you before, is the inner truth of the Creator. The physical world is the place for it to be utilized, revealed, and reveled in."

"All right, that I can understand," David said, "but how can you say it about Israel?"

"Because," the rabbi answered, "Israel is the

manifestation of the inner hope of G-d when He created the world. It was the name G-d intended to bestow on the human being who would attain His highest aspirations for mankind. And that is why the renaming of Jacob to Israel[23] is one of the most significant events in history?"

"One of the most significant events in history?"

"Yes. It wasn't just the calling of a name. Jacob was the culmination of all Abraham's efforts and hopes. The climax of Jacob's life was the revelation that he was to be called Israel, because that renaming was the realization of all the forefathers' efforts.

"Jacob was first called Israel when he wrestled with the angel of evil. Israel, the Torah tells us, means 'he who has striven with [the agents of] G-d and man and has prevailed.'[24] That encounter serves as a symbol for the mission of Israel — till the coming of the Messiah, the children of Israel would have the mission to tangle with and outlast evil in all its manifestations.

"'Israel' is really a crown. G-d waited to bestow it on the human being who would rise above all humanity. Jacob, building on the efforts of his father and grandfather, was that human being. Therefore, his earning of the name 'Israel' was not just a personal, local milestone but one with implications for mankind and even the universe.

"Therefore, when Jacob was named 'Israel,' an era was closed. G-d fused the name Israel, and the mission implied by its name, with the offspring of Jacob. Before him, theoretically, any individual or family could have made themselves worthy and claimed the mission. After him, however, there could be other individuals, families and nations, but only the descendants of Jacob could call themselves Israel.

"At Sinai, the name — the mission, the ideal — of Israel was wedded with the offspring of Jacob. From that point on, all others who would want to identify with G-d's highest ideal would first have to align themselves with the ones whom G-d said exemplified that ideal. Individuals from outside the seed of Israel were and still are capable of awakening themselves, searching after the truth, and attaching themselves to it. Nevertheless, true pursuit of G-d's ideal is only found in the destiny and mission of Israel.

"A solid piece of evidence supporting that is the fact that the Christian and Moslem religions claim the Jewish mission for themselves. They say the 'Old Testament' was true at one time but has since been superseded. Their founders knew that the only way they could possibly hope to legitimize their claim would be to first acknowledge Israel's election as the group assigned to carry out G-d's mission and then claim it was somehow bequeathed to them.[25] Nevertheless, the die was cast and the foundation laid long ago. 'Only in your fathers did G-d delight, and He loved them and chose their offspring after them, namely you, above all peoples, as it is today.'"[26]

"Therefore, Torah is not the only unique message of Judaism; Israel also is. Yes, Jews are not perfect, however, as Israel we are the ones whom G-d gave the mission of wrestling with the agents of evil head on. In the end, like Jacob, we will prevail over evil. That is G-d's promise. Now, however, while we are in the midst of this battle it is not clear that we will prevail; and therefore it is not immediately clear how unique among the peoples we are. However, G-d waits for us, only us, because our forbearers earned the title Israel, and Israel is a people whom G-d deemed worthy of undertaking the mission for which G-d created the world.

"All the world's a stage for the blossoming forth of these two concepts: Torah and Israel. The two go hand in hand. Torah is the electricity, and Israel the lightbulb. Only Torah can make Israel shine. And only through Israel is Torah, the resplendence of the Creator, revealed in this world.

"When all of Israel will shine forth with the light of Torah in its full beauty in the days of the Messiah, the mission begun by Abraham will be complete. Then all the nations will see how creation was meant to be in the beginning. They will thank and admire us for being different throughout all the centuries of persecution. It will not sound strange to them to hear that the Jewish people are a chosen people and that the world was created for Israel."

The Root of Anti-Semitism

"Rabbi, wouldn't you say that ideas like the chosen people create more anti-semitism?"

"You are probably right. In fact, this is the root of anti-semitism, namely: G-d gave all mankind an opportunity. However, only the three forefathers pursued G-d's ideal absolutely and thereby earned the privilege to be chosen by G-d. Esau, Jacob's twin brother, by contrast, lived a life antithetical to his grandfather Abraham's ideal.[27] Therefore, no one more than Esau, the offspring of Abraham and Isaac — the first two forefathers — could possibly have felt the failure of that lost opportunity.

"Rather than changing his ways, Esau deepened his indulgence in evil and convinced others, who might have otherwise attached themselves to Jacob's ways, to partake in his hatred. His greatest 'success' in this regard was his grandchild Amalek, whose hatred was so fanatical that his descendants sacrificed everything in a senseless and vain attempt to destroy the children of Israel in the desert, after they were taken miraculously out of Egypt! Although unsuccessful in that respect, Amalek did succeed in injecting their venomous, baseless hatred into others. That venom runs in the veins of society today.

"Nevertheless, remaining true to who we are despite anti-semitism is one of the tests of a descendant of the forefathers. If not for the influence of evil in the world, there would be nothing very great about remaining true to the good.

"The irony about anti-semitism is that while the anti-semite is jealous because G-d chose us, many, many Jewish people try their best to deny that uniqueness. They think it is prejudice to consider oneself part of a privileged people. However, being a Jew is more of a responsibility than a privilege. 'I, G-d, have called you to righteousness . . . and have set you up as a covenant of the people, for a light unto the nations.'[28]

"Our problem is that we don't appreciate who we are, we don't know who we are. We want to be so good that we don't want to think that we are any different, that we have a certain calling which is unique in the world. We are different, though. And it is important to us as well as the world that we live up to who we are and not worry that others will see us and ridicule us for being different."

Twain on the Jews

"Rabbi," David said, "I can't argue with you when it comes to the Torah. Nevertheless, are Jews really different? Can you put a Jew next to a non-Jew and see any difference?"

"I'm not saying I can always see the difference. However, there is a difference. And I think, in retrospect, historically speaking, an objective observer will have to agree that Jews have always been significantly different from non-Jews."

"How can you say that, though? You are not an objective observer. Being Jewish, rabbi, you are biased."

"Would you call someone like Mark Twain biased?"

"Mark Twain?"

"Yes, Mark Twain, the great American writer. Did you ever read what he said about the Jews?"

"No."

The rabbi walked over to his bookshelf and removed a pamphlet. He flipped a couple of pages and said to David, "Here is an excerpt from Mark Twain:

"'If statistics are right, the Jews constitute one percent of the human race. It suggests a nebulous, dim puff of star dust lost in the blaze of the Milky Way. Properly, the Jew ought hardly to be heard of; but he is heard of, has always been heard of. He is as prominent on the planet as any other people, and his commercial importance is extravagantly out of proportion to the smallness of his bulk. His contributions to the world's list of great names in literature, science, art, music, finance, medicine, abstruse learning, are also way out of proportion to weakness of his numbers. He has made a marvelous fight in the world, in all the ages; and has done it with his hands tied behind him. He could be vain of himself, and be excused for it. The Egyptian, the Babylonian, and the Persian rose, filled the planet with sound and splendor, then faded into dream-stuff and passed away; the Greek and the Roman followed, and made a vast noise, and they are gone; other peoples have sprung up and held their torch high for a time, but it burned out, and they sit in twilight now, or have vanished. The Jew saw them all, beat them all, and is now what he always was, exhibiting no decadence, no infirmities of age, no weakening of his parts, no slowing of his energies, no dulling of his alert and aggressive mind. All things are mortal but the Jew; all other forces pass, but he remains. *What is the secret of his immortality?*"[29]

"Now," the rabbi said putting down the pamphlet, "the truth is that Mark Twain is only one person, and he probably wrote that without appreciation of our greatest 'contributions' to the world — our accomplishments in Torah and other triumphs of the spirit. Nevertheless, the flourishing of Jewish accomplishment throughout history — not to mention the miracle of our mere survival — is a phenomenon that only one who chooses to be blind can deny.

"David, the bottom line is that a Jew is different. A non-Jew is free to pursue his or her own righteous lifestyle or examine ours and convert, but not to live the Torah as a Jew."

"But why? Why can't anyone keep the Torah? If keeping commandments are the measure of performing G-d's will, why is a non-Jew limited to only seven?[30] Can't a sincere non-Jew take on eight or nine or 613 commandments, for that matter? Aren't they more righteous for taking on more?"

"No. It is only better to do what G-d's will for you is. G-d's will for the Jew is 613 commandments, no less and no more; His will for the non-Jews is seven commandments, no less and no more. Taking on anything other than what G-d's will for us is, is a denial of G-d. It shows that somewhere on the inside, one's motivations for keeping the commandments are suspect and tainted."

Cindy Speaks Up

Cindy decided it was time for her to interject her thoughts. "Rabbi," she said, "I've been sitting here quietly and listening, but now I have to speak up. I am genuinely interested in Judaism, independent of my feelings for David."

"Are you so interested that you would be willing to never see David again?"

"Never again?"

"Or at least completely sever contact with him for a year or so to allow each of you to find your own paths, truly independent of each other?"

"Why should I?"

"Because you never know what, deep down, motivates you. Maybe you are interested because you are in love with a Jew or maybe you equate being Jewish with prestige or some other benefit."

"And let's say I was ready to sever contact for a

while?"

"Then I am required to ask you: Why are you interested? What do you need Judaism for? You can be a good non-Jew and keep seven commandments. Why would you want to start worrying about keeping 613 commandments?"

"Because of what I've read and discussed with David."

"From the outside looking in, it may appear interesting, but being a Jew means you have to be willing to pay the price."

"Please explain to me what you mean by that."

"I don't know what anyone else has told you or what you have read, but if you really are sincere, then the first thing you should consider is that if the Messiah does not come soon, you take the risk of being placed on a line to be gassed and burned for your Jewishness just as we were a few decades ago. If you are not ready to do that, then converting is not worthwhile for you."

Cindy took a long look at the rabbi. "That's a horrible thing to say. Do you want to scare me off?"

"No. It is very simple. It is the truth. I am a holocaust survivor. The Jews in pre-Hitler Germany were in a better position than Jews in any country today. Germany had been one of the first countries to 'emancipate' the Jews. Jews had assimilated into the society and contributed greatly to Germany's rise as an economic, political, military and industrial world power. Furthermore, the German people were regarded as the most civilized, morally refined and cultured people. None of that prevented the holocaust from originating in that very country by those very same people.

"Nowadays, the State of Israel alone receives so much negative attention from every corner of the world that no Jew anywhere dares feel even as secure as pre-Hitler German Jews. I have seen both worlds. Only a Jew who lives in a bubble does not consider the possibility."

"If that is true, rabbi, then how do *you* deal with the hatred?"

"I have to because G-d made me a Jew. If I was born a non-Jew, why would I try to get myself in all that trouble?"

"What about all those reasons you gave David? What about the mission of a Jew? You must really believe it otherwise you could easily live like most other Jews who have assimilated."

"First, I know that the Nazis didn't discriminate between assimilated and religious Jews. They searched back numerous generations to find if you had Jewish blood. In fact, Jews who thought they were good Church-going Christians were taken and thrown into the camps. Throughout all Jewish history, up till our day, G-d always made sure to remind the Jew that he was a Jew no matter how far removed he was; and if the Jew did not do so himself, a Hitler did it for him. So, it doesn't help to assimilate.

"Secondly, you are right. It is not just an obligation for

me. I know what a Jew is, and possessing that knowledge, I wouldn't trade it for the world. For the same reason, not only I, but my parents, my grandparents and their grandparents extending back more than 2,000 years have dealt with the prospect of hatred and death because we all knew the value of being Jewish. In fact, the hatred of others only proves it to us more. We have something of true value which makes them jealous."

"What is that something?"

"To make it simple, the answer is eternity — and not just a self-proclaimed eternity, but an eternity guaranteed and inscribed over and over again in the Torah. And what other nation's history can support that claim like the Jewish one? After all, we Jews survive while the 'thousand year' Reich is dead. We Jews are here, and Spain's infamous Inquisition is known only from history books. We Jews are around, and where is the Roman soldier who murdered our ancestors, destroyed our Temple and laughed when we told him we are eternal and he temporary? They hate us because we don't merely talk about eternity; we live it and are living proof of it."

"Your people may live on, but aren't you afraid of losing your own life?"

"On an individual level, as well, we have always known of the Torah's guarantee that all Jews have a unique share in eternity.[31] Only the body dies. The one who does not see beyond the limits of a material life feels great anguish from even the slightest reminder that the body will perish. On the other hand, the one who knows he is eternal does not suffer when separated from the body, even when that separation is brutal.

"How can I deal with our long history of persecution?" the rabbi said. "It is because I, and my people have always remained focused on the fact that we are eternal parts of an eternal entity. It is in our consciousness that the end goal is the life of the spirit, not the life of the material body."

"It makes sense to me," Cindy responded, "but why can't a non-Jew also focus on the life of the spirit, as you say, too, and attain the same degree of closeness to G-d as a Jew?"

"For one reason, because, generally speaking, non-Jewish religions, at best, only talk about spirituality as something divorced from physicality.[32] Their highest ideal is to totally transcend the body and soar into the heavens. The Torah ideal, on the other hand, is not to get high — to lift the spirit out of the body — but rather to bring the heights down into man, to make the person down here into a physical being who lives a heavenly, eternal existence even while he breathes. The Jew, through his Torah, ideally lives a life of the spirit while immersed in a full physical life."

"It sounds like a contradiction."

"That is precisely the point: it is not. The physical

need not be a contradiction to the spiritual."

"But, practically speaking, how can a person be immersed in the physical and remain focused on the spiritual?"

"Only through G-d's own instructions — the Torah — which outlines for us how to do so. While demanding that we eat, marry, interact with others and generally take part in a physical life, the 613 commandments force us, every single day, to make choices between the material and the spiritual — every single day. For instance, I wish to eat whatever I want, but the Torah tells me to only eat *kosher*. I want to hoard money and possessions, but the Torah commands me to give and give and give. Fifty . . . one hundred . . . two hundred times every day, we are asked to give up a part of our stake in the material world.

"This is a training which keeps us focused on the life of the spirit even while we engage in the physical. And the greatest of our people is no different from the simplest in this regard. All must partake of the physical. That is not a concession; that is the ideal. I don't believe any other major religion or philosophy claims that; and if they do, they certainly don't have the Torah, which is the detailed guide given to man by G-d for fulfilling that ideal."

A Soul Linked to Eternity

"Rabbi, that helps clear up a lot of things for me," Cindy said, "but you have only convinced me more about my decision. I am not just willing to keep the Torah; I would want to of my own volition. I would not just be doing it to keep David. True, I love him for who he is and have only more respect for him showing so much interest in his heritage, nevertheless, as he became more interested in Torah, I resigned myself to losing him. Yet, by remaining non-Jewish and keeping the Torah, here is a novel solution that can satisfy everyone."

"Everyone, except the G-d of the Torah, Who forbade it," the rabbi said.

"Maybe my problem," Cindy continued, "is that I can't see anything wrong in keeping an authentically Jewish home and remaining non-Jewish. I mean, just because it happens to be that my mother was not Jewish, does it make sense to say that I can't fulfill the laws? I can shop for only *kosher* food and keep *Shabbos*. I can do anything a person born from a Jewish mother can. In essence, what is the difference between a Jew by birth and a non-Jew?"

"Being Jewish is not essentially ethnic. It is not even merely religious, because it entails more than adherence to an ideal and a lifestyle. It starts with a unique orientation of being.

"Hopefully, that orientation becomes manifest in a person's actions. Even if does not, however, a Jew possesses a unique soul. After all is said and done, a Jew by definition is that species of mankind who lives his life as if this physical world is not an end in itself."

"What about all the Jews you and I both know who are not so spiritually oriented, self-sacrificing and idealistic? Are they still Jewish?"

"Yes."

"But they don't even seem to be committed to keeping the Torah's ideals superficially."

"At the core, even they are. It's just that they have layers and layers of impediments preventing the light of truth from reaching down to their heart."

"How do you know?"

"That is the meaning of being a descendant of Abraham, Isaac and Jacob. The Torah theme of crowning the forefathers with the name Israel in effect tells us that G-d blessed the physical offspring of Abraham, Isaac and Jacob with a soul linked to eternity. This makes the Jewish soul specially oriented toward the idea that life in this world is not an end in itself. Individuals may not yet have actualized that potential, however, all people born of Jacob's seed automatically possess a soul bound to the eternity of Israel, whether they have actualized it or not."

"How do you see that?"

"Just take a look around today," the rabbi replied. "Even a casual observer can't help but notice that Jews are disproportionately involved in every manner of idealistic scientific, political, philanthropic or other type of movement. Remember the quote from Twain I read to you before. It is as true today as it was then. As genuine offspring of the forefathers, we as a collective whole, are not satisfied with a world bent on pure materialism and moral mediocrity. We are simply not happy in the pursuit of the material as a pure end.

"Admittedly, unaware of the true value of Torah, many well-meaning but non-Torah-imbued Jews will substitute a little higher level material pursuit for the true ideal enunciated in the Torah. However, if they knew what their Torah said, and examined it honestly, they would see that their ideals are like mere idols compared to the objective of serving the one true G-d in the Torah way.

"Inside, though, whether he realizes it or not, a Jew cannot be satisfied with finite ends. That is because deep down, even independent of his or her affiliation to keeping the Torah, a Jew's soul is aware that G-d chose it for a higher mission. That awareness orients it toward the ideal that life is more than just living for the sake of creation itself; life is for living for the end goal of creation. And that subtle nuance in orientation makes all the difference."

Stewardesses and Passengers

"Maybe I don't yet understand exactly what you mean by this orientation. What do you mean that life is for living for the end goal of creation? Can you please explain it to me a little more clearly?"

"Yes. Did you ever fly in a plane?"

"Yes."

"Where did you go?"

"Rome."

"Did you pay for the ticket?"

"Of course."

"Did you realize that on the same flight was someone just like you who did not have to pay for the ticket?"

"What do you mean?"

"The stewardess. You and she looked and dressed similarly, but you paid to be on the flight, and she not only flew for free but even got paid for flying."

"Yes, but she worked for the airline."

"Exactly. And that is the real difference between a Jew and a non-Jew."

"Please explain."

"Both the stewardess and the passenger occupy the same cabin, but are completely different in orientation. The end goal of the stewardess is to service the plane; the end goal of the passenger, on the other hand, is to use the plane to get from one point to another.

"When the plane lands, the stewardess could just as easily go right back; she does not see beyond her immediate goals on the flight. In fact, remove the pay, and she will quit. To the passenger, though, the destination is everything. It is so important that she is willing to pay a high price for the ticket.

"Creation is like the plane," the rabbi said. "It is a vehicle to a higher end; as an end, it serves no purpose; it only acquires purpose when it is used as a vehicle to that higher end.

"The non-Jew's highest end is to serve the vehicle itself; his seven commandments only deal with things that help the material world run smoothly: don't steal, don't murder, set up courts, etc. However, beyond the physical world running smoothly, like the stewardess once the flight has landed, inside he doesn't really care, he has no real goal.

"The Jew, however, deep down knows that this world is a vehicle to reach eternity. That knowledge is burned so deeply into his soul that he is willing to pay the highest price. He possesses a character which at any moment is ready to sacrifice material comforts, and even his life if need be. If his physical seat is comfortable, fine, but if not, he realizes this world is only a vehicle to a higher existence. The destination is everything.

"Being a Jew is by no means a free ticket," the rabbi added. "A Jew pays a heavy price and does not appear to have any advantage over the non-Jew. He has to keep many more commandments. He is restrained in his pursuit of the material. He is persecuted and hated. A Jew who understands who he is, though, should be happy to pay a high price. Because he pays such a high price, if nothing else, it shows that he is living for the destination. If nothing else, this indicates that he is paying for his ticket.

"Being Jewish means having, somewhere inside, a sensitivity toward eternity. To bring out this otherwise latent sensitivity, we are placed in a world where things of a temporary nature are very attractive — so much so, in fact, that we can become distracted from our goal of bringing to fruition our latent sensitivity toward eternity. As I said, the price of eternity is the willingness to part with the temporary. And as I told you before, nothing like the Torah exists which trains a person to release his stake in the temporary. Torah draws out and molds the Jewish soul, whose essence is already uniquely linked to eternity."

"And if a non-Jew, who you say doesn't have this link, decides to keep Torah, what happens then?"

"It is like gasoline without a car. In order to be able to reach its destination, a car needs two things: a working engine and gasoline. Torah is the gas. Israel, the individual whose soul is forged in the mold of the forefathers, is the engine.[33] A genuine convert gets that engine. Without the engine, though, keeping the Torah does not get the non-Jew anywhere. It is like having gas without an engine. In fact, gasoline by itself is a volatile, fume-producing substance which by itself is dangerous to human life. So, too, a non-Jew who takes on the Torah."

"And what is the status of those Jews who do not keep the Torah?"

"It is like a car without gas. As a recipient of the

unconditional promise G-d bestowed on the seed of Abraham, Isaac and Jacob, a person born from a Jewish mother can never lose his status as a Jew. Nevertheless, without Torah a Jewish soul cannot reach its destination. It is a car without gas."

"But what if a person was never taught the Torah," David asked. "How can he be blamed?"

"That is a good question, and no one can know the answer for sure. All we know is that G-d does not do anything unjust. In the end, we will see and understand the reasons for everything: why this one was born at that time; why another one was given a different set of circumstances, etc.

"In spite of it all, in the final analysis, a Jew who is ignorant of Torah, and does not keep it, is a tragedy. He or she is like a passenger who is unaware that his parents paid for his ticket and put him on the flight. He even slept through the take-off.

"Now, all of a sudden, he wakes up and finds himself buckled into a small seat. He doesn't know how he got there and where his destination is. Even though he will end up in the same airport as a passenger who has that information, he is very unhappy not knowing how he got there or why he should continue. All he will be able to see is his immediate discomfort, while feeling jealous about the stewards and stewardesses who seem to be able to do almost whatever they want, and get paid for doing so!

"Furthermore, the passenger who wakes up in the middle of the flight will naturally reject the attitude of those passengers who seem to be content with the restricted living conditions. What he doesn't know, however — and what the contented passengers do know — is that he is heading toward a fantastic destination which offers him more than anything he can have in the cabin of the plane.

"Not researching his past, however, he may even mock and ridicule the passengers who reveal to him that there is a destination and that the destination is a wondrous, wide, far-off place. As long as he remains unconvinced or uninformed, he may even deny he will ever land safely; as a consequence, he may jump out of his seat, wreak havoc, or buy drink after drink — anything to avoid facing life in the seat. He may spend all his money on alcohol and movies or use it to buy a more comfortable seat or even get the idea that he can invest in a section of the plane, which in reality he can never own.

"Meanwhile, the passengers who know and value the destination are busy readying themselves; they do not spend too much of their energy and resources on the flight itself. Every moment they spend, whether it is sleeping or planning an itinerary, is ultimately calculated to improve their stay once the flight lands. When the plane finally does land, they walk out fresh, happy and excited; they head straight for the exits which will take them to the wondrous land.

"The uninformed passengers, however, will stumble out of the plane, in varying degrees bewildered, tired, penniless and in a drunken stupor. They may even have come to consider themselves as stewards and stewardesses and want to get on the first plane back. In either event, they will not be in nearly the same condition as those who understood well the purpose of the flight, and who conducted themselves accordingly.

"The analogy is fruitful, and I can go on, however, my original intention was to illustrate to you how a Jew and a non-Jew may look the same, but have entirely different orientations. If G-d forbade their union in marriage, both of you have to realize that the differences are significant and critical."

"You've made your point well," Cindy said. "At least I understand now that there are underlying rationales for the Torah taking such a stance. I have one more question I want to ask you before leaving: A non-Jew can become a Jew, and even an unaware Jew is Jewish because of the connection to the forefathers of Israel, but why can't a Jew ever convert to being a non-Jew?"

"Can a passenger become a stewardess in the middle of a flight?"

"I guess not. But, on the same note, can a stewardess become a passenger in the middle of the flight?"

"Theoretically, yes. All she has to do is pay the price of a ticket."

Aftermath

The conversation ended cordially, with Cindy thanking the rabbi for his time. Shortly afterward, David and Cindy both agreed that it was best to stop seeing each other, at least temporarily. For a while, David kept in contact with the rabbi, who always expressed his admiration for the courage he had to follow through with an intellectually informed decision, despite the emotional backlash. Of his own volition, David eventually went to Jerusalem to learn Torah. The rabbi was not sure, however, what happened to Cindy.

Almost a year later, the rabbi was in his study when the phone rang. "Hello . . . Oh, Hello! Yes, of course I remember you, David. I am so happy to hear from you . . . no, it's not a bother at all. How have you been? . . . That's great news. When your learning goes well, everything else seems to fall into place. I can tell you will make a big impact on your people one day . . . What's that? . . . You're engaged? Mazel Tov! Mazel Tov! Who is the girl? . . . I can't believe it. Not the same Cindy? . . . You mean you didn't know that all along that she had converted? . . . That's unbelievable . . . It would be my honor to come to the wedding. Just send me an invitation . . . Yes, I look forward to it."

The wedding was a true Jewish affair, filled with energy and emotion. When Cindy, who had now officially changed her name to Ruth, saw the rabbi for the first time in more than a year she could barely contain her excitement. She thanked him, telling him how at first she thought he had been a little too strong for her, but in the end realized his forthrightness was the best and only way he could have dealt with the situation. She wanted to tell him more, but it was not the time or place. Finally, she told him, "If you want, use my story, and if anyone asks, tell them the bottom line is that this stewardess decided to pay for the ticket."[34]

PART II

CHAPTER 1

ON THE HIGHWAY

"What a surprise!" the rabbi exclaimed. "Come in. It must be at least a year since I last saw both of you."

"A year and a half to be exact," David said with a smile.

"You've been married a year and a half already?"

"Yes."

The rabbi offered them a seat and a hot drink. Then he said, "Seeing both of you, the way you are, is a great inspiration for me."

"Thank you."

"Rabbi," Ruth said, "before we go any further, I just want to say that we're sorry we haven't kept in such close contact."

"There's no need to apologize," the rabbi said. "I don't

mind. Why should you? It tells me that you've both been very busy."

"Yes, we have both been very busy growing over the past couple of years," David said.

"I can see it on your faces," the rabbi remarked. "Before anything else, though, why don't you catch me up a little about what has been going on in your lives?"

"That's a good idea."

David and Ruth spoke animatedly of their wedding and *sheva brachos*, and then briefly about some of the other details concerning their lives. Afterward, David leaned forward and said, "Rabbi, we are happily married. Furthermore, we have really integrated well into the community. We blend in. We know a lot of the nuances, etcetera. For all intents and purposes, at least in other peoples' eyes, we have made it. It's a dangerous thing, though, to 'make it.'"

"What David means," Ruth spoke up and said, "is that we don't know if we are growing as much as when everything was new to us."

"Yes. I suppose it was to be expected," David added, "or maybe not; I'm not sure. In either case, speaking for myself, the thing that bothers me is that sometimes I find myself pressured and just fulfilling obligations. Sometimes I don't have a feeling for things I know I should have feeling for."

"I don't know if this will make you feel any better," the rabbi answered, "however, that is common.

Beginnings are filled with many of those magical, one shot breakthroughs. The challenge is to sustain, maintain and extend the beginning.

"Furthermore," the rabbi added, "the problem is not only for returnees to Torah like yourselves. It is the problem as well for those who were raised in observant households. I call it becoming a robot Jew. It is an affliction none of us are immune from."

"I suppose that is comforting," David added, "however, we don't want to be robot Jews. Why is it so easy for things to become routine?"

"Probably because of the demanding nature of living as a Torah Jew. Torah is a vivifying, holistic program of life covering every particular situation one can think of. The problem is that while involving ourselves with the particulars, we can come to forget about the whole.

"It is like going on a long drive: Before departing, you look at a map and make note of all the different roads and highways you will need to take. Once on the road, however, you need to keep your eyes on the road, looking out for appropriate signs and exits which keep you on course. Periodically, though, it is necessary to take a look at the map and remind yourself where you are and where you have to go.

"On the highway of life, too many of us too often forget to do the latter. We are so busy with the road immediately in front of us that we tell ourselves we don't have time to stop, pull over to the side, take out the map and make sure we are not on the wrong road. That is the way life can become fragmented; we fulfill our obligations and forget to look at the map. However, taking the time to look at the map and see the greater picture can reassure us about our expenditure of energy on the immediate particulars. That usually is the whole difference between being a robot Jew and a Jew energized by his obligations."

"Practically speaking, what does it mean to look at the map, and what can we do now?"

"First, you have no choice but to keep on growing. You have to do everything you have been doing — learn as much Torah as you can, do as much *chessed* as you can, live in an environment which supports your efforts, etc. — and, in addition, you have to make sure to periodically stand back and remind yourselves about the larger picture. You have to work on developing your life's philosophy.

"You see, within the Torah framework, each of us can develop a unique outlook which enhances everything we do. The clearer and fuller our personal outlook, the better we can relate to the specifics of our daily lives.

"I don't think enough people really appreciate how important that is," the rabbi continued, "particularly in our times. Most Jews no longer live in insular little villages which were soaked through and through with Torah values and ideals. Back then, even the simplest people could not help but be effected by the Torah atmosphere of their surroundings. They took for granted their knowledge of the larger picture which we, nowadays, usually have to work hard to obtain. In today's fast pace lifestyle, if you don't take the time to develop your personal Torah outlook, you are almost sure to get lost in the details.

"In any event, the idea is to plug yourself into activities which can increase your clarity of perspective. Make the effort to read appropriate Torah books, listen to Torah tapes at home or in the car, and attend Torah classes and seminars. Make sure you set aside time to do that. That is the medicine for surviving our times."

"Rabbi," David responded, "I understand what you are saying, but sometimes we are just so exhausted."

"You have to know your limits. You have to pace yourselves. However, my point is that the more you understand what you are doing and why, the more energized you will feel doing whatever it is you have to do. Taking one step backward to see the larger picture can help you muster the energy to take two steps forward.

"We were not made to be robots," the rabbi continued. "We can't go on when there is no heart in what we do. We have to do what we have to do, and inject it with heart. With a new understanding or simple reminder about what it means to be who you are, the very same effort you employed yesterday will be more effective."

"Life without Torah is certain death; Torah without life, though, is also a type of death. In order to be a true Torah Jew, in order to pass it on to your children, it must be a *Toras chaim*, a Torah of life. You must derive vigor and energy from the demanding lifestyle of living the 613 commandments."

The phone rang. The rabbi spoke on it for a couple of minutes, hung up and returned to the conversation. "I wish I could spend more time with you now," he said, "but I have another appointment, and tonight I am giving a lecture which I still have to prepare for. Perhaps if you come to the lecture tonight, we can talk afterwards."

"We would love to," Ruth said.

"But," David quickly reminded her, "we are only in town for a short while. No one would like to go more than I, but I don't think we have the time."

"Isn't something like this exactly what the rabbi meant that we have to make the time for?"

David thought for a moment and turned to the rabbi. "What's the topic of the lecture?"

"Life," the rabbi said with a smile. "I know that sounds general, however the truth is that while it is the most obvious and probably the most often-spoken-of topic, it is also the most obscure and least understood topic. Although we literally breathe it twenty-four hours a day, we don't know what it is, what to do with it, and how to take advantage of it."

"That sounds like the conversation we had when I first came to your office a couple of years ago," David said.

"That's right. And I will probably talk about many of the same things we spoke about back then, except now you should be able to understand and appreciate it on a deeper level. The framework of your Torah outlook is more together now.

"The lecture is designed to help you strengthen and extend that framework. It is really about everything we were just talking about: how understanding the larger picture — what is the purpose of creation, what is a Jew — is vital information for fully living your everyday life."

"Is it for beginners?"

"Not specifically. The majority in the audience will probably not be beginners."

"I guess," David said, "from everything I've told you, it sounds exactly like what I might need to hear."

"What we might need to hear," Ruth added. "David, I would really like to attend. Everything else can wait. Isn't something like this lecture exactly what we came here for?"

"I guess you're right. Where is it, and what time does it start?"

CHAPTER 2

THE IDEA BEHIND CREATION

The lecture hall, which had been sparsely filled when Ruth and David arrived, was now almost full. Most of the audience were observant Jews, although a young man without a *yarmulke* happened to sit down next to David. David engaged him in a conversation. Before they could really get far, though, the rabbi took to the podium and began speaking:

What is life?

That question is so often repeated, so broad, and so many different people have tried to answer in so many ways, that we look askance at anyone who tries to tackle it. For Torah Jews, however, we have a definite guide for answering that question. Our Torah is called a tree of life; it is life. The question for us is: What is Torah? How is it life?

The answer to that, unfortunately, is not always well-understood.

A human being builds a house because he has a need for shelter, and even more so, he has a need to feel rooted — he needs a home. The house is a means to producing the idea of home. If people neglect the idea of home while busying themselves with building the house, they undermine their original intent. That is because a house is only the means for building a home.

How many people do we know, and how many stories of people have we heard, where they enslave themselves to careers in order to move into a beautiful mansion, but neglect their marriage, their children, their very selves? It is a human pitfall we all have to guard ourselves from: losing sight of the goal while involving ourselves with the means.

So, too, when G-d created the world, He had an underlying intention. The idea that G-d had an underlying intention is worded in the language of the Sages as follows: 2,000 years before the creation of the world, G-d wrote the Torah.[35] The Torah preceded creation in that it was the idea behind creation. It is the primordial knowledge of existence. It is the idea to which life is nothing more than a means.

What do I mean that life is nothing more than a means? G-d is eternal, and the temporary nature of the physical creation is contradictory to eternity. Creation, therefore, is not an end in itself; it is a means. It is a means for giving the part of creation made in the Divine image — mankind — the opportunity to earn a share with *Hashem* in eternity.

How many of us, though, neglect the end goal of Torah in our headlong rush to survive and thrive in life? How many of us, while erecting the structure, forget the idea? The answer is almost all of us to some degree, and too many of us too often to a greater degree. And therefore we have to constantly ask and remind ourselves: What is life? What is Torah? Who are we? And what are we living for?

Even as Jews committed to Torah, if we do not sharpen our focus on the answers to these questions, we risk severing our lifeline to the real purpose for which we were created. And once we sever that lifeline we begin to lose the vitality and inner drive that were intended and are, indeed, necessary to the task of building the outer structure.

Now, in addition to telling us that Torah preceded the world by 2,000 years, the Sages also tell us that the world was created to last 6,000 years: 2,000 years of void and desolation (*tohu va'vohu*), 2,000 years of Torah, and finally 2,000 covering the times of the Messiah.[36]

The 2,000 years of void and desolation lasted from the creation of Adam until the year 2,000 when Abraham was 52 years old. The 2,000 years of Torah encompassed

the lives of the forefathers, the giving of the Torah on
Mount Sinai, the life of King David, the building of the
Temple and its destruction, the flourishing of the Oral
Torah through Ezra, the building of the Second Temple
and its destruction, and ends roughly around the time the
Oral Torah was redacted and written down in the form
known as the *Mishnah* by Rabbi Yehudah HaNassi. The
era of the 2,000 years of the Messiah coincides with the
long exile which we are still currently in the midst of.

How do exile and persecution represent the era of the
Messiah? That will have to wait for another lecture.[37]

Our goal in this lecture is to first understand the
purpose of creation and how it became manifest in
history. In other words, how did mankind implement the
idea behind creation, G-d's Torah, which existed '2,000
years before the world,' in the first 4,000 years of
history?

Rather than just a brief overview of the spiritual
history of the world, however, there is a more immediate
goal in discussing this topic. That goal is how can we use
this overview of the purpose of creation for our practical,
day-to-day lives? What can you take home with you
when this lecture ends which can change or help
energize your life?

And let's admit it: we do need to be energized. How
many Jews wake up in the morning, look at their non-
Jewish neighbors, and wish they were them? How many
observant Jews are there like that? How many times has

that Jew been us? The physical and spiritual persecution has taken its toll on us. Let's admit it.

Poor or wealthy; married or unmarried; childless or overburdened with children — all of us, to some degree, walk around as if under a heavy, heavy load. However, imagine we were told that in the 'load' was something equivalent to a sack of diamonds. How differently we would think about the burden on our back!

So, too, the one answer to all our problems is the knowledge that being a Jew is like carrying a heavy load of diamonds. Yes, it can seem burdensome at times, and yes those without the load may laugh or pity us as we go along. However, when we finally reach home, all the diamonds will be ours. Then, those who cast off the burden, or never had it to begin with, will not laugh so loudly. They will not pity us. We will pity them.

The Jew is that entity chosen by G-d to use his gift of life to gain eternity — doing that despite the temptation to live for the immediate pleasure. Through this service, the Jew teaches the rest of mankind its purpose, gaining eternity himself and influencing others who might want to join him in becoming a partner with G-d in eternity. Therefore, the purpose of creation and the definition of a Jew are one and the same topic. Through examining creation, we find out why G-d needs Jews; through gaining knowledge of who a Jew is, we deepen our understanding of the purpose of creation.

CHAPTER 3

WORLD HISTORY IN A NUTSHELL

Imagine you had a desire to build your business into a huge, international company with branches in every major capital city.

Big businesses today need computers. Therefore, the first thing you have to do is design and have written a computer program, customized for your needs. This computer program, this piece of software, is in reality your step-by-step plan encoded in a computer programmer's jargon, for carrying out your original desire. The software has to have every possible contingency and detail written into it.

Only once the software is written is the next stage possible — finding the piece of hardware, the actual machine. The hardware cannot be acquired until the software is complete because the hardware has to have the power, speed and capacity to handle the software. And until you have the software in your hands, you do not know exactly what that is.

Thus far three steps have been enumerated: the original desire, the plan written up as software, and the hardware.

The next step should be installing the software into the hardware. However, something needs to be done before that step: you need to hire a proven computer operator who is capable, responsible and reliable. Putting the operation into the hands of anyone less than completely qualified can be disastrous. Therefore, even before installing the software, it is necessary to advertise and see which candidates will step forward.

One by one, the candidates will apply. Each one needs to be screened and tested. Capability, capacity, durability, dedication, honesty, etc. — you can only hire the one who possesses all these characteristics.

After finding the right candidate the process is still not complete. The person needs to be trained. And the training has to be thorough and challenging. Only after all this do you actually install the software into the hardware.

As an added measure, in order to insure that the worker works with the highest motivation, some type of profit-sharing motive needs to be employed. The worker needs to have the opportunity to become a partner so that when he does the job well, he benefits, and when he does not do the job well, he suffers. This will insure the highest performance.

This is the spiritual history of the world in a nutshell.

G-d's Desire

G-d had a desire. Exactly what that desire is, no one knows — at least not yet. The Messiah is not here. And we cannot truly understand G-d's desire until it is finally realized — until the coming of the Messiah. However, because the world is here, we can say that G-d had and has some desire in creating it, even though we do not exactly know it.

The Software of Creation

So, G-d had a desire.

The next stage entailed mapping out that desire in full; in other words, writing the software. The Torah is the software. That is what is meant by the statement that the Torah existed 2,000 years before the world. The entire plan is in it — everything.

When I say everything, I mean everything — as our Sages said: 'There is nothing missing from the Torah.'[38] Not only the universe and the planet Earth, but every human being who was, is, and will be; his birth, his death, his family, his job; his height, weight, hair color, eye color — everything, even his telephone number and social security number! All are in the Torah — and from there they all get their existence.

How is that possible? If we would have the spiritual microscope to penetrate into the depths of the mystery of the Torah, we would find everything. As it is, only the Master Programmer knows all the intimate details and how everything fits — only the One who wrote the software can see it clearly.

The Codes of Creation

Nevertheless, certain true Torah giants, who endeavored to understand the operation at the level of a programmer, have unraveled some of the mysteries encoded in the Torah. This is really the topic for another lecture, The Codes in the Torah,* however, to give one illustration: Maimonides, known by the acronym Rambam, (the first initials of **R**abbi **M**oshe **B**en **M**aimon), lived approximately 850 years ago, long after the Torah was written. One of the great medieval rabbis had said that the Rambam was hinted to in the following verse of the Torah (Exodus 11:9): "Now, G-d said to Moshe, 'Pharaoh will not heed you in order that My marvels may be multiplied in the land of Egypt.'"

How is the Rambam hinted here? First, in this verse, G-d is addressing Moshe (Moses) which is the Rambam's first name as well. Second, it was in Egypt where the

------

*   See the Appendix with the article <u>Back to the Future</u> by S. Ornstein for background information on the "Codes."

'marvel' who became known to the world as Maimonides flourished. His works in Torah, philosophy, and medicine are marvels of the intellect, and have gone a long way toward multiplying the greatness of G-d's name in the same way the miracles in Egypt performed through Moses enhanced G-d's name. Third, the last four Hebrew words in that verse read: *'Rivos Mophsai B'eretz Mitzraim,'* — 'My marvels/ may be multiplied/ in the land of/ Egypt.' Taking the first letter from each of these words, Maimonides' acryonym, RaMBaM, is spelled out.

That is interesting enough, however, there is more.

Rabbi Michoel Dov Weissmandel, who passed away in 1957, developed the hobby as a young man of counting letters in the Torah in order to uncover hidden codes. Convinced that there were codes embedded in this verse which hinted to more details of the Rambam's life, he decided to study the passage.

Starting from the first letter *mem* in the word Moshe (which is both Moses' and Maimonides' name) he counted fifty letters. Why fifty? Rabbi Weissmandel had been discovering codes of fifty laced throughout the Torah.[39] Fifty is a symbol of Torah; the Torah was given by G-d on Mount Sinai fifty days after leaving Egypt. For these reasons, as well as others I do not have time to elaborate on now, the number fifty is significant.

Rabbi Weissmandel started counting every fiftieth letter from the *mem* of Moshe in the verse where the Rambam is hinted. Sure enough, he found that every fiftieth letter spelled out the word 'Mishneh.' Rambam's major work is the entitled the 'Mishneh Torah.'

Rabbi Weissmandel continued his count in hope of finding the word 'Torah' encoded every fiftieth letter. And indeed he did, just nine verses later, in verse 12:11. In the Hebrew word *et* of that verse, he found the *tav* of the word 'Torah,' which was spelled out every fiftieth letter from that point. Therefore, starting from the verse where it was stated that the Rambam was hinted to, a fifty letter code of 'Mishneh Torah' was found.

Coincidence? The skeptic might say, "The word 'Torah' was not encoded right next to the word 'Mishneh.' There is a gap of several verses between these two encoded words." However, the gap makes the nature of this find more incredible. For, from that original *mem* in Moshe — which is the same *mem* which begins the word 'Mishneh' — to the *tav* of the word *et* in verse 12:11 — which is the *tav* which begins the words 'Torah' — there is a gap of exactly 613 letters. The 'Mishneh Torah' is an elucidation of the 613 commandments written by the Rambam.

One has to remember that all of these allusions emanate from the verse which has the acronym RaMBaM, and a statement to 'Moshe' about the 'marvels' in 'Egypt.' If that were not enough, the entire section where these allusions are found conveys information about the preparation for Passover on the night of the fourteenth of the month of *Nissan*. The fourteenth of *Nissan* was the Rambam's birthday.

This is only a small taste of what is meant that everything is contained in the Torah. With the help of computers — which Rabbi Weissmandel did not have — many, many incredible codes have since been found. The probability that these codes should occur at all, and then that they should occur in relevant locations, is astronomical; furthermore, nothing like it has been found in any other document. Only the Torah has it, because only a document by G-d could have such unimaginable depth.

As I said, if we had the know-how we could find not only the Rambam but everyone, including you and I, as well as everyone who has ever lived — all in the Torah. But this lecture is really for another time.

The Hardware of Creation

Everything is in the Torah. It has to be, because it is the software. What is the hardware? What is the means of bringing out the information contained in the software? Creation. If Torah is the software, then creation, the world we live in, is the hardware.

'G-d looked into the Torah and created the world.'[40] Through creation, the inner idea of the Torah is made palpable. Thus, creation signifies the next stage is the process of bringing G-d's original desire to fruition.

Hiring the Operator

With the software written and the hardware to match secured, the next stage was to find a computer operator. This 'computer operator' would need to be the most capable and responsible person available. He could not be forced or coerced into applying for the job, because only someone who would be dedicated to the project of his own volition would make a qualified candidate.

Therefore, G-d waited for one sterling individual to step forward. He 'waited' because having chosen to give man free will He was dependent, so to speak, on that individual to step forward on his own. G-d therefore waited.

During the first 2,000 years of the world, only a handful of candidates stepped forward. Of those candidates, only two, Adam and Noah, warranted serious consideration. However, neither of them, for various reasons, met all the criteria.

Then Abraham stepped forward.

Through the chaos of his times, Abraham saw the beauty and design of the world. He realized that the chaos was really an organized chaos. Destruction was followed by construction. There was a rationale to the chaos. This told him that someone or something was running the world.

This understanding led Abraham to become the world's greatest searcher. He searched and searched. He tried every idolatry, psychology, fad and philosophy to try to get to the root of existence. Finally, he discerned that only One Power was behind everything — G-d, the Creator of heaven and earth, the Mover of time and history.

The Difference Between Abraham and Noah

Now, of course, Noah also knew the world was not chaotic, and that there, indeed, was a single G-d to whom he had to listen and obey. Why wasn't Noah as privileged as Abraham?

To put it simply, Noah was a good worker; he put in his time and was productive. However, he was not really interested in anything more. What am I accomplishing for You, G-d? Am I responsible for the whole world? He never entertained these questions like Abraham did.

Abraham, too, was a good worker. Then he went beyond that, though. He wanted to make himself a partner.

"G-d," he said, "You obviously have an interest in this world. Please let me know what it is. How can I serve You so that it should be a success? What good is it if I do my job and other people don't do theirs? I want to take responsibility to try and make everyone do his job. I don't want to just serve creation; I want to work to fulfill Your purpose in creation, whatever that may be. I want to make the creation a success for Your sake."

When Abraham reached that level of understanding, G-d in effect said, "Ah, you are the first volunteer who has grasped the root idea behind this computer operation called creation; you are the first one who shows Me he is interested in taking responsibility for every facet of this world. If you are genuinely interested, though, I have to test you and see what price you are willing to pay. You have to go through a training period which will challenge you in every respect. If you pass this, I will share My dividends and profits with you. You will indeed become a partner with Me.

"Of course, those dividends are not anything ultimately related to this finite world. They are part of the eternal world. Therefore, if you pass My tests, I will make you a partner with Me in eternity. And that is only fair, because My purpose in creation is an eternal purpose. If you only pursued things related to the finite creation, I could not reward you with anything but finite rewards. But if you are truly devoted to the purpose of creation, then your reward will naturally be eternal."

We know that Abraham was given ten tests.[41] These ten tests parallel the ten statements with which the physical creation, the hardware, was made.[42] The hardware, though, needs software, and the software is the ten commandments. Abraham's ten tests were intended to parallel and link together the hardware with the software, the physical with the eternal, creation with the Torah.

(Pharaoh, by contrast, who denied G-d, was given the ten plagues (*makkos*) because he denied the existence of the software. By punishing him with the ten plagues it was a lesson to those Jews immersed in Pharaoh's culture that the purpose of life is to convert the potential of the ten statements into the eternity of the ten commandments.)

In any event, the ten tests were part of the trial period which was necessary before installing the software into the hardware. Abraham would have to prove himself a selfless, devoted 'computer operator' before the installation could even be considered.

Of course, devotion and concern outside the self proved ultimately to be the distinguishing factor of Abraham. Noah was righteous, but with limits; he was righteous 'within his generation.' Abraham's righteousness was unlimited because he was not happy with his own righteousness. He wanted the whole world, including his generation and all future generations, to be righteous. And he wanted this not for himself, but for G-d's sake — to fulfill G-d's purpose in creation.

The Purpose of Creation

What, specifically, is G-d's purpose in creation that Abraham grasped and dedicated his life to? The truth is that we cannot know G-d's true purpose in the ultimate sense. However, at the very least, Abraham taught us one thing: our purpose. A human being's highest purpose is to live completely for G-d's purpose. In essence, it is to make the world aware that there is a

G-d and that He has a purpose. In the words of the prophet, it is to fill the world with the knowledge of G-d.[43]

This is really the idea of *kiddush Hashem*, literally, 'sanctifying the name (of G-d).'[44]

The Torah opens: 'In the beginning G-d created the heaven and the earth. And the earth was desolate and void . . . .' The first verse mentions heaven and earth together. This intimates that the elements of these two realms, heaven and earth, were similar. Just as heaven is spiritual, eternal, and filled with the presence of G-d, so, too, was the earth originally. In other words, at creation even the physical was permeated with the presence of G-d.

Then the second verse tells us that a change took place: 'And the earth was desolate and void . . .' This intimates that G-d, so to speak, withdrew Himself from the earth — from the physical — leaving only the subtlest, most minimal suggestion of His presence.

Later, after the creation of man, G-d commanded the man to "be fruitful and multiply, and *fill* the earth and conquer it."[45] This does not only refer to the commandment of bearing children, spreading across the globe and taming nature. Every thing in the physical realm has a spiritual counterpart, and the spiritual counterpart of this command is the command to fix up the desolation and void stated in the second verse. In other words, it is man's purpose in life to 'fill' the hollow caused by G-d's withdrawal. Wherever G-d's presence seems to be lacking in this world, on this earth, man's job is to recognize G-d's presence. Doing so fixes the lack; it fills the hollow.

In Hebrew, the word for a hollow is *chalal.* The Zohar points out that *chalal* is the root of the word *chilul,* meaning desecration. The appearance that the world is devoid of its Creator is called *chilul Hashem*, desecration of the name of G-d. The opposite of *chilul Hashem* is *kiddush Hashem*, sanctification of the name of G-d.

In these first two verses, then, the purpose of life is mapped out. The earth — the physical, material world — originally possessed eternity and spirituality, i.e. G-d's presence, no less than heaven. However, G-d hollowed out the earth of His presence to give it the appearance that it can run independent of Him. He did this in order to give mankind the opportunity to make *kiddush Hashem* and, thereby, put G-d's presence back in the world the way it originally was.

Someone can ask: What is gained by simply restoring the earth to its original state?

The answer is: partnership. G-d is not anything that we can really effect or change. He lacks nothing. He is omnipotent. He is G-d. The process of restoring the earth to its original spirituality is, therefore, not for His sake, but for ours, because by doing so, we become partners with G-d in eternity. In other words, even though the world after the Messiah will be nothing more than a restoration to the world at creation, the world after the Messiah will be a world created, in part, with the free-willed input of you and me.

That ability is represented by the choice between *chilul Hashem* or *kiddush Hashem*, the choice to sanctify or desecrate G-d's name. This is where our free will lies: G-d's name can be constantly on our lips and near to our heart or very far. The cultivation of that awareness or its neglect is in the hands of mankind. Therefore, the human mission is to replace the emptiness of *chilul Hashem* — i.e., the denial or absence of awareness of G-d's presence in the hearts of mankind — with the knowledge of *kiddush Hashem* — the awareness of G-d's presence. That is why we were created.

This mission has a time limit, though. When G-d withdrew His presence, creating the chalal, the earth was like an empty container. Although filling this container would take thousands and thousands of years, it — like any container — can (and will) eventually be filled.

Picture an hour-glass. The sand in the top half is the knowledge of G-d; when G-d originally withdrew His presence from the earth below, He stored it, so to speak, above. The sand is flowing into the bottom half of the hour-glass, though — the knowledge of His presence is filling up the world. When the last granule of sand will finally drop into the bottom half — when this earth will be filled to the brim with the knowledge of the presence of G-d exactly as it originally was — then the purpose of creation will be complete.

Each human being since the beginning of creation is responsible for a certain quantity of granules. Each *kiddush Hashem* a person performs — each heightening of the awareness of G-d a person produces — contributes to the overall goal of creation. Thus, making *kiddush Hashem* is the personal mission of each of us.

And this is what Abraham came to realize on his own. He was born into a world where G-d was emptied from the heart of man. The ten generations of Adam to Noah had culminated in the Flood. The *earth,* as the Torah tells us, was literally filled with corruption.[46] The people of Noah's time did not mind hearing or talking about G-d, as long as He remained in heaven and did not deter them from the unabashed pursuit of their material yearnings.

From Noah to Abraham, another ten generations passed. When Abraham was forty-eight years old, the world was undertaking the project to build the Tower of Babel. At first glance, this seemed like a noble generation who were pursuing a noble undertaking. After all, the generation of the Tower of Babel was unique. Mankind had unified like never before. They had one language and a single purpose of truly global proportions — to build the Tower of Babel. Why were they punished? Why did G-d disrupt their plans and their unity?

Because their goal to reach 'into heaven' was only in

order 'to make themselves a name.'[47] That seemingly innocent statement reveals their true intentions: They sought to build a tower into the heavens in order to remove G-d from there and put themselves in His place. In other words, with the building of the Tower, they intended to, once and for all, wipe out the awareness of G-d from the forefront of human consciousness so that no more would the lips of man be a mouthpiece for the praises of the name of G-d. Their goal in building the Tower was the ultimate *chilul Hashem*.

Returning to the metaphor of the hour-glass, the generation of the Flood sought to stop up the hour-glass; they did not seek to replace G-d with themselves, but to make a separation between heaven and earth (with G-d in heaven and man in control of earth). The generation of the Tower, though, sought to wipe out G-d from heaven — to knock off the top of the hour-glass and get rid of the sand for good.

Abraham was bred and raised in the generation of the Tower. Just as they possessed *chutzpah* — just as they had the audacity to seek to remove G-d from heaven and put themselves in His place — Abraham, too, possessed *chutzpah*. However, he inverted the *chutzpah* and used it to seek to remove from their heart the denial of G-d and replace it with genuine belief in His Almighty Presence.

This was the status of the world after the first twenty generations. Whether the generation of the Flood or the generation of the Tower, the goal was the same: an attempt to frustrate G-d's purpose in creating the world, to create and maintain *chilul Hashem*. Abraham learned to operate in this vacuum.

As an aside, our world today is witness to the co-existence of the motivations of both generations. In the west, materialism drives society. G-d is not really denied, but rendered irrelevant. As long as G-d and religion do not stand in the way of fulfillment of personal desire, they can be given lip service. Not surprisingly, then, crime, drugs, immorality etc. are symptomatic of today's west no less than the same societal corruption present in the generation of the Flood.

On the other side of the world, the communist dream corresponds to the dreams of the generation of the Tower. Material desires, its excesses and by-products, are not foremost in the peoples' consciousness and tabloids. Ideas like a classless society where everyone is equal, unity for the sake of building the communist vision, etc. motivate human behavior. Communists talk about the highest ideals . . . as long as they can remain atheists, though. The truth is they want to replace G-d with themselves. They want to rebuild the Tower of Babel.

The world we live in today is witnessing the climax of the philosophies of these two generations. As Abraham's descendants, our task is to convert the drive evidenced in both the materialists and atheists into the drive for *kiddush Hashem* and true recognition of G-d.

Collectively, we have to be the Abraham of the modern age.

To return to the main theme: In the time of the building of the Tower of Babel, Abraham's perception of G-d had, without outside influence, matured. From the darkness of a world bent on *chilul Hashem*, Abraham came to the conclusion that the purpose of life was to make *kiddush Hashem*. Thus, G-d made Abraham the first of the three forefathers, who would become known as the family of Israel. Israel in turn is that group of people, descended from the three forefathers, whose being is intrinsically oriented toward making *kiddush Hashem* — who have been given the keys to fulfill the purpose of creation.

The truth is that until Sinai, *kiddush Hashem* was an intangible concept. The forefathers had learned exactly what it meant to make *kiddush Hashem*, however, the idea was, as of yet, not defined well enough so that generations and generations of their descendants would know exactly how to go about sanctifying G-d's name.

And the idea of *kiddush Hashem* does need to be defined.

The Moslems think, among other things, that jihad, or holy war, is a sanctification of G-d's name. The Christians, too, burned at the stake, murdered, robbed and exiled millions and millions of Jews (as well as others) through the centuries, all in the name of the love of their deity. So much hatred, bloodshed, and barbarity have been perpetrated in the name of jihad, crusade and the 'love' of G-d that it is no wonder that so many people perceive G-d and religion in a negative light.

They point out that more people have died in the name of religion than anything else. This is their rationale for closing their minds to anything which has to do with G-d. That is the effect *chilul Hashem* can have. False ideals perpetrated in the name of G-d can do more to frustrate G-d's purpose in creation than anything else.

Obviously, *kiddush Hashem* needs to be defined. How can we sanctify G-d's name? Is there a way we can turn even the so-called mundane aspects of our everyday life into an affirmation of G-d's presence, so that every moment is a potential *kiddush Hashem*? G-d knew that would be our question of course, and, from the beginning, therefore, He intended to give mankind His Torah, which would lay out in detail all of the behaviors and attitudes which would make every moment of life a potential *kiddush Hashem*.

Installation of the Software

Before giving the Torah, however, G-d waited for the family of Israel to develop. Why did He wait? Because the giving of the Torah is equivalent to the installation of the software. And until a tested and true operator would be found to run the computer, the installation serves no purpose, and would in fact be dangerous for the well-being of the overall operation.

And, therefore, G-d took Abraham and gave him an Isaac. He took Isaac and gave him a Jacob. He tested Jacob and eventually found him worthy of the name Israel.[48] He then took the family of Israel and forged them into the nation whose sole purpose would be to produce *kiddush Hashem.*

Now, why did the forging of the family Israel into the nation Israel have to take place under the oppression of Egypt, the nation where idolatry, immorality and brutality were without equal?

The answer is that G-d wants the *whole* world to be filled with knowledge of Him — even and especially the lowest parts. Therefore, in order to prepare the national entity called Israel to be the spreaders of *kiddush Hashem* to all nations throughout all the ages, their initial formation had to take place amidst the nation who were the lowest of the low, that nation most obscured in the darkness of the times. There they would get the training necessary to prepare them for the real task of being a light to the nations till the very end of days.

Egypt is called the 'Iron Furnace'[49] because the Jewish experience there served to remove the dross from the ore; it burned into the Jewish soul forever a deep abhorrence of the lifestyle of the Egyptians — which was unparalleled immersion in materialism, idol worship, bloodshed and immorality.

It was like an immunization shot. Just as an

immunization is the introduction of the disease into the system for the sake of building a resistance to the disease, so, too, the exile in Egypt. It infused into the Jewish soul forever its distaste for materialistic, man-made pursuits. Even though individual Jews would always have the free will to deny and overcome that distaste, the national character of the Jewish people was forged in the Iron Furnace of the Egyptian exile.

The experience in Egypt, however, was all for one purpose: To prepare the nation of Israel for the experience on Mount Sinai. There they would receive the Torah, the definitions of how to make *kiddush Hashem* — the laws detailing the behaviors, attitudes and lifestyle which would help them mirror on a national scale the behaviors attitudes and life of Abraham, the one who first realized that the whole purpose of life was to dedicate himself to pursuit of *kiddush Hashem.*

The nation of Israel, then, was and is an extension of Abraham. And the giving of the Torah, therefore, is the next stage in the Divine plan of creation — the installation of the software into the hardware. Only after this national entity was tested and purified, and found to be possessing all the necessary qualifications, was it time to actually commence the operation. Only then was G-d prepared to install the software — the Torah, His idea behind creation — into the hardware.

The Purpose of the 2,000 Years of Torah

Abraham turned fifty-two years old in the year 2,000 from creation. During the next 2,000 years — from the maturing of Abraham's vision to the lives and development of his family to the exile in Egypt to the giving of the Torah to the entrance into the land of Israel to King David to the building of Solomon's Temple and its destruction to the building of the Second Temple to the flourishing of the Oral Law under Ezra to the destruction of the Second Temple and the writing of the Oral Law — one theme is constant: the spread and proliferation of Torah.

For sure, there were lows as well as the highs. The ten tribes completely perverted themselves and had to be severed from the body of Israel; the Temple was destroyed because of shortcomings of the people. However, generally speaking (and certainly in comparison to the previous 2,000 years of chaos and void) the Torah and the G-dly ideal were advanced through those middle 2,000 years of Torah.

The height of these 2,000 years was the era of Shlomo HaMelech, King Solomon. In his time, not only did the nation become the economic and intellectual center of the world, but the structure which would house the *Shechinah,* the 'Presence' of G-d, was finally erected.

The *Bais Hamikdash* (the Temple — that structure) was considered one of the wonders of the ancient world. More than its architectural wonders, any person could go there to see and feel the presence of G-d. Whether it was the ten daily miracles,[50] the other-worldly sounds of the Levitical singers, or the presence of prophets and prophetesses, as well as other types of holy people, both scholarly and simple, the *Bais Hamikdash* was a place where G-d was made palpable. Praise and awe of His Holy Name came easily to the lips of anyone who beheld the site. It was truly the fruition of the ideal of *kiddush Hashem*.

Despite all this, through the 2,000 years of Torah, one important ingredient for fulfilling the purpose of creation was missing.

Abraham had discovered G-d and made *kiddush Hashem* in the complete absence of G-d's presence. He grew up in a world devoted to making a name for themselves. There was no room for G-d. When Abraham found G-d and dedicated all his strength to spreading and sanctifying His name, he did so in a spiritual vacuum.

For most of the 2,000 years of Torah, climaxing with the *Bais Hamikdash* of Shlomo HaMelech, the *kiddush Hashem* generated by the proliferation of Torah did not come about in a spiritual vacuum — G-d gave the Jewish people a land, a national identity; He performed miracles; He related His desire to His prophets. The accomplishment of making *kiddush Hashem* was due only in part, to the input of the people of Israel — G-d very much openly supported their efforts.

Therefore, with the close of the 2,000 years of Torah, the 2,000 years of the times of the Messiah began. They would be years of darkness, persecution, exile and the seeming abandonment of the Jewish people by G-d. Nevertheless, the chaos of this 2,000 year period, which we are still in the midst of, would have a purpose — it does have a purpose. It is the final stage of the process of filling the whole world with the knowledge of G-d. It is the stage where the chore of *kiddush Hashem* is almost exclusively, if one could say so, in the hands of man.

The presence of G-d is obscured. There is a spiritual void. Yet, it is that very void which gives us the opportunity to complete the purpose of creation in a way even those who lived in the glory days of the *Bais Hamikdash* were not privy to. We have the ability to be like Abraham and declare G-d's presence in a world where that presence is greatly obscured.

This, then, is the dynamic operating behind the suffering of the Jewish people. Suffering is a darkness; it is a fact of existence which contradicts the existence of G-d. The children of Israel have been sent out on a mission to make *kiddush Hashem* wherever He is denied, wherever darkness now reigns.

Israel suffers more than any other nation or people because our mission is to enter the thick darkness of *chilul Hashem* and turn it into the brilliant light of *kiddush Hashem*. And the more we do so, the more significant the accomplishment of filling the whole world with the knowledge of G-d.

This test of the 2,000 years of the Messiah is like the stage after the 'computer operator' has been selected and trained, and even after the software has been installed. There comes a point where the master programmer has to let his employer/partner run the operation on his own, without any overt input. Yes, he secretly watches from the sides to make sure nothing totally disastrous happens. However, for the most part he allows the operator to make his mistakes, and to pay for his mistakes.

The world we live in, despite its technological and scientific advances, is in reality a place covered in darkness. The darkness is the absence of the knowledge of G-d. Yet, the more dark and hollowed out a place is, the more brilliant the light when *kiddush Hashem* is introduced. That understanding is the key to surviving and thriving in the 2,000 years of the times of the Messiah — may his light be revealed soon.

The truth is that this is not the real subject of this lecture. In order to build the foundation necessary to fully appreciate the lecture about the times of the Messiah, the times we live in, it is important to return to the specific topic of this lecture: understanding the purpose of life, and using it to make our own lives vital, meaningful and ultimately Jewish.

CHAPTER 4

HOW MUCH IS A MOMENT WORTH?

The idea that *kiddush Hashem* is the purpose for which we were created is completely alien to the outside world. The outside, generally, has no idea what the purpose of life is. A case in point is the phenomenon of celebrating birthdays.

What is the justification for celebrating birthdays? Does it make sense? Think about it. Why do we make birthday parties?

Imagine a man was condemned to death by the courts. Seeing him devastated by the final verdict, the judge tries to calm him, "Don't worry. Before we put you in the electric chair, we will put you in a train which will stop at eighty stations. And at every station, you can have a party."

"Thanks, but no thanks," the condemned man would probably say.

He has no choice, though. They put him on the train and there is no escape. Does it make sense that this condemned person should celebrate at every station? Each station is one stop closer to the electric chair.

We are the same way. The minute we were born, we were sentenced to die. Each year is one station closer to the end. And there is no escape. Is it a consolation that we are allowed to make a celebration at each stop?

If anything, the reverse would be appropriate: make a mini-funeral. We could hear sixty or seventy eulogies before it is over. That might be consolation.

I told this to an audience once and someone responded by claiming that the real reason we make birthdays is because it is really a sad day. In order to drown out the sadness, we make a party. Unfortunately, the statement was more true than that person suspected. For many people, the definition of good living is forgetting about the fact that he or she is alive.

All unhappiness in the world is due to the fact that people do not know what the purpose of life is. That is a serious statement, but I think that when you think about it you will see that it is true.

How is *all* unhappiness the result of not knowing the purpose of life?

Because happiness is not an end. It is a result of working toward a purpose. If people pursue it as an end, it escapes them because by focusing on it as an end, they automatically are losing focus on whatever true 'end' they must actually pursue to be happy. When you pursue happiness, you lose it; when you pursue a goal, you naturally feel happy, motivated, and whole. Therefore, when one knows the purpose of life and pursues it, happiness is truly attainable.

However, most people do not know the purpose of life. They don't even know it exists. And, therefore, they don't know what they accomplish by living.

I often ask my audiences: How much would you pay for a moment of life? Usually there is one sharp businessman present who answers, 'It depends on how much money you can make in a moment.' Time is money, the saying goes. In other words, time in itself is nothing; if it is used to earn money, then, yes, it has worth.

Of course, other people will answer that life is priceless. Yes, a moment of life is priceless. But just how much do they mean that?

Let's say you were offered the option of extending your life an extra moment. However, to get that extra moment, you had to give up your life's savings, including whatever money you may have saved for your children and loved ones. Would you do it?

Probably not. After all, most people say, what can you accomplish in a moment? At the very least, it would be a tough decision.

How could that be a tough decision, though? Those same people said just before that a moment of life is priceless.

The answer is because most people don't really believe it. Most of us do not really know what we accomplish with a moment of life.

This is where knowing the purpose of life and being dedicated to it not only would make you opt for that extra moment of life, but will vitalize and rejuvenate all the moments starting right now.

What is the purpose of life?

The real end goal of life is to serve G-d through filling the world with the knowledge of G-d, to reveal G-d through the very essence of our life — to make *kiddush Hashem*. If that is one's goal, then every moment — every means — becomes an end.

If we understood this, then we would value our time very differently. For instance, let's say you worked an entire week, cashed your check, and on the way home got robbed. You would feel terrible. An entire week of work was just wasted. That's the way you feel if you deep down believe that time is money.

However, if you went to work that week because you know that G-d put you in the workplace to be a living example of G-dliness, a Torah Jew, then your week was a smashing success. The money? G-d gives it and takes it away.

How much is a moment worth? It depends. If you

think in terms of the temporary, then the moment is only temporary. It delivers you immediate gratification which you enjoy for about sixty seconds. After those few seconds, it will never return. If, on the other hand, you know that every moment possesses the prize of eternity — the potential to fulfill life's purpose and create *kiddush Hashem* — then the moment is not a few seconds, it is eternity.

How does one know what is temporary and what is eternal? The choice is not always obvious to our untrained mind, especially considering the fact that all human beings have a great ability to rationalize. The only satisfactory answer, then, is that G-d told man what is for eternity and what is not. "I put before you a blessing and a curse, life and death — choose life!"

Each of the commandments in the Torah points us to blessing, life and eternity. Exactly how is eating *kosher* or putting on *tefillin* a choice of eternity? That we don't necessarily see right away. We are 'computer operators' extending back in a long line to the first computer operator, Abraham.

We are not G-d; we are not the Master Programmer who knows exactly what punching each key produces. All we know is that we have instructions in front of us. The instructions are the commandments of the Torah; they are the screen prompts which tell the operator which key to push next. As long as we push the right keys, even if the act is totally meaningless to us, it produces its desired effect.

Of course, that does not preclude the fact that we can experience great meaning in the act of fulfilling the commandments. However, feeling immediate fulfillment with each commandment should not be our criterion for doing it. If every moment is another opportunity to punch another key, and by pushing that key we are producing everlasting reward, then this moment is not a few seconds, this moment is eternity. That knowledge, alone, is enough to make life meaningful and happy.

Of course, the choice is not easy. The price of eternity is the willingness to sacrifice temptations of the moment. I often explain this with an analogy. Imagine you are holding the last apple in the world. You are so hungry, though, that you decide to eat it. You temporarily satisfied your stomach, however you just destroyed the last chance to replenish the world with apple trees.

So, too, each moment of life is a potential seed. If you consume it for your own gratification your eternity will be barren. If you are willing to forgo your temporary pleasure, however, and you plant the moment then your eternity will be plush and fruitful. As we say in our daily prayers, '. . . You gave us a Torah of truth, and eternal life you *planted* in our midst.'

The more a Jew knows what he gains by keeping the Torah, the less of a sacrifice it becomes; it becomes the greatest of pleasures. Torah gives us the opportunity to make each moment purposeful. Knowing our purpose produces true happiness, even when the purpose for that moment is withdrawal from some immediate gratification. When we understand the value of a moment, we won't trade it for anything; we will fight for every moment of life. That is the unique message of the Torah's definition of the purpose of life.

Life and Death: A Case in Point

Let me illustrate this by relating to you a true story. A couple of years ago, an 18-year-old young man learning in a *yeshiva* in England came down with cancer. He became so sick that his doctors told him that chemotherapy wouldn't work; they advised the family to take him home from the hospital in order to live out his last days in peace. The boy was very sick.

The family didn't give up, however. They brought him to America and found a medical center not far from my home. In fact, the family ended up staying at my son-in-law's house.

The doctors told them that they had an experimental therapy which, although very painful, might extend his life by a couple of months. The doctors insisted, though, that they would only go ahead with the therapy if the patient signed a paper taking full responsibility for the procedure.

The parents, in turn, asked a great Torah authority whether their son was allowed to or even obligated to take on this therapy. He mulled over all the details and told them that, in their particular case, the only one who could make the final decision was the son himself.

Shortly afterward, the father called me up and told me his son wanted to speak with me. The boy asked his parents to step out for a short while in order to speak to me alone.

"I know I am going to die soon," he told me, "And I have no complaints against G-d, even though I don't understand why this situation came upon me. I am not afraid. The thing that bothers me most is that my family will be pained. However, if this is what G-d wants I accept it wholeheartedly.

"Nevertheless," he continued, "I have been told about this therapy which may extend my life an extra month or so, and that the decision to take it or not is completely up to me. My question to you is: What am I accomplishing by living an extra month? I am already helpless, lying here connected to all these tubes; I can't concentrate more than five minutes at a time to fulfill any *mitzvos*. My family will lose a son, but wouldn't it be inflicting more agony on them by seeing me in this state for an extra month? What should I do?"

First I told him that I hoped he didn't expect me to make the decision for him. He concurred. Then I told him the only thing I could perhaps do was to educate him how much living an extra month was worth. If he understood how much it was worth, then, he could make a better, more informed decision.

"Okay," he said.

"In the entire Torah," I asked him, "which of the commandments is the greatest?"

"The greatest?"

"Yes."

"I don't know."

"The greatest commandment is the commandment to 'live by them (i.e., the commandments).'[51] Life," I told him, "is the greatest commandment because the commandment to 'live by them' tells us we must transgress the Torah if a situation arises where keeping a commandment puts our life in danger. If you are on a deserted island and you can only survive by eating pork, not only are you permitted to eat it but you are obligated to do so."

I then went on and related to him a discussion in Torah law which, although hypothetical, sheds light on this issue.[52]

"Imagine," I told him, "an old person in a vegetative state on his death bed in the hospital, and doctors guarantee the family they can extend his life one extra moment, but the procedure requires that every Jew in the world transgress all the commandments — excluding murder, adultery, and idolatry, which are the three exceptions to the commandment to 'live by them.'

"I know it is completely hypothetical," I told him, "but imagine such a case, and we get confirmation that the doctors' claim is legitimate; instead of dying at 100 years of age, by all Jews transgressing 610 commandments, the old person in the vegetative state will die at 100 plus one moment. What does Torah law dictate in such a circumstance?

"The answer is that not only would it be permitted to transgress in that case, but one must transgress to add on that extra moment.

"This Torah law," I told him, "is revealing to us how much a moment of life is worth. G-d is telling us that even though He created the world so that we could keep all the commandments in the Torah, if even one person — even in a vegetative state — can gain one extra moment of physical life through temporarily suspending the fulfillment of those commandments, then He prefers we suspend them. That is how valuable a moment of this life is to Him.

"Take a deep breath," I told this young man. "King David wrote: Every soul (*neshama*) thanks G-d. By vowelizing the second word differently the verse can be read: Every breath (*neshima*) thanks G-d. Every breath of air is an extra second of life, and a second of our life gives G-d unimaginable things.

"Think about it. A second of our life gives G-d unimaginable things.

"We, G-d's creations, don't necessarily comprehend what G-d gets by our living, but we know He must get tremendous things if He is willing to have virtually His entire Torah transgressed to gain a moment of life. A single breath with this awareness is the song of the life, even if that life may be experiencing unbearable pain or existing in a vegetative state.

"You ask me," I told him, "what can you accomplish by extending your life an extra month? I ask you: Do you realize how much G-d is willing to sacrifice so that you should live an extra moment?

"I am not telling you what to do," I said, "but deciding to take on the extra therapy is a declaration to the world that life, in any form, is the most precious gift. You would be showing us how a person about to lose life is willing to pay the highest price possible for more life.

"After all, you would not be doing it for yourself, because you are not afraid to die; and you would not be doing it for your family, because they only suffer more by seeing you in this state. You would be doing it only because G-d told you, through the Torah, what a moment of life is worth *to Him*. It is a declaration to G-d that a few more breaths to thank Him is your real purpose for living.

I told the boy, "Unfortunately, many of us are simply existing; we complain about all the things wrong in our lives. We are insensitive. We don't really know what life is. We don't appreciate the value of a moment. However, since you have no other choice but to face reality, and fight for every moment of life, you can teach us about life. And, if you do that, I envy you — you are my teacher."

In the end, he made the decision to take the therapy. A few days later, his father came to me excitedly and asked, "What did you tell him? What did you tell him? He is always smiling. The doctors can't get over how well he takes the therapy. They ask me if I know why. I told them that he's been like this ever since he talked with you. Rabbi, what did you tell him? Did you hypnotize him or something?"

I assured the father that I did nothing more than teach him the Torah outlook on life.

Now, this boy was very sick, as I said, but to the doctors' surprise, during that extra month, he became well enough to take leave of the hospital for a couple of weeks. He ended up staying at my son-in-law's house. I visited him there, and he explained to me that sometimes when he got severe pains he could not concentrate enough to remember what I had told him. He took out a tape recorder and asked me to repeat everything. He also wanted to include, on the tape, answers to some new questions which had since come to his mind.

For instance, one question was that, as the *Talmud* tells us, even the most evil of evil people do not suffer in *gehinnom*, the Jewish concept of hell, more than the equivalent of twelve months. Yet, he asked me, he was already into the thirteenth month of his illness.

My answer to him was that in *gehinnom* you are cleansing your soul; here, in this life, you are expanding your soul, you are making your soul more of what it is.

This life is a time of producing; in the afterlife you reap, but you do not sow new seeds. That is why the *Talmud* says that a moment of life here is worth more than the entire existence in the afterlife. When he heard this, a huge smile came across his face.

After a couple of weeks, he had to return to the hospital. He listened to the recording constantly. The doctors and nurses couldn't understand how he was always so happy. They didn't realize it, but his secret was that he truly appreciated life.

On the Sabbath before Passover he left this world, but even then it was with a smile on his face.

True happiness results from the awareness of converting every moment into a fulfillment of the ultimate purpose. This young man converted breath after breath from this life into eternal life while right here! And that is really the goal of Torah — to teach us how to bring eternity into our otherwise temporary lives.

Reacquiring Moments of the Past

Every man, every woman plays a vital role in the fulfillment of the overall plan of the universe. When we pool all our talents into the fulfillment of this plan, we not only experience our own sense of fulfillment but we, so to speak, give G-d great pleasure because we fulfill His purpose. And that produces a cycle of happiness and meaning which can turn every moment of life into a potential end goal.

The question some people ask, however, is let's say from now on I am aware that I can get meaning out of each moment. What about all the moments I did not utilize? How can you expect me to feel excited when so much of my life is behind me, and I did not use that life to fulfill the Torah? If I started today, I would be like a one day old?

That is a legitimate fear. In order to quell it, though, I relate a story from the *Talmud*.

There was a man named Elazar ben Durdaya who dedicated his entire life to the pursuit of attending prostitutes. One time, he was told mockingly by one of them that his G-d would never accept him. Something inside snapped. In a moment of deep remorse, he ran away and sat down on a rock. Distraught, he sought consolation and advice from others, but soon he realized that he was getting nowhere.

Finally, it dawned on him, that everything depended on him alone. Elazar ben Durdaya then sank his head between his knees and started crying profusely until, the *Talmud* tells us, his soul left his body. A voice from heaven said, 'Happy is your lot *Rabbi* Elazar ben Durdaya. You attained your everlasting world.'[53]

One moment earlier, he was Elazar ben Durdaya the great sinner, and the next moment he not only earned his ultimate reward but even earned the title Rabbi! The *Talmud* concludes that when Rabbi Yehudah HaNassi heard this, he cried and said, 'There are those who acquire their world after many years of hard work, and there are those who acquire it in one moment.'

Now, let me ask you: Let's say Elazar ben Durdaya was ninety years old when this happened. Only in the last moment did he become Rabbi Elazar ben Durdaya. How old was he when he died?

Since he lived ninety years so contrary to the way he died, the natural answer would be that he was one second old. However, the truth is that he died as a ninety year old Rabbi Elazar ben Durdaya. He converted ninety years worth of sins into ninety years worth of merits!

How is that possible? It is a tenet stated in the *Talmud* that while anyone who returns to G-d out of fear has his sins forgiven, anyone who returns out of love not only has them forgiven but has those sins converted into merits![54] Love of G-d turns sins into merits because the person who wants desperately to return to G-d realizes that his sins are obstacles standing in the way. He becomes embarrassed, disgusted and distraught over them. This feeling propels the person to move as far away from them as possible. The sins become the fuel upon which the fire of love of G-d is kindled.

To earn the title Rabbi, Elazar ben Durdaya must have converted his lifetime of sin into good. That is possible only if he returned to the right path out of love of G-d.

In order to drive this point home further, let me relate

an incident concerning one of the holy men of this century, a man who was known for his overflowing love of humanity.[55] Possessing the reputation as a miracle worker whose prayers really worked, people constantly flocked to his door in order to have him say a prayer for them.

This rabbi would ask the person in need to tell him one good thing he had done. The rabbi would use that good deed and say in his prayers, "Master of the Universe, this person is keeping *kosher* or *Shabbos* or whatever — You have to save him." One time, a person asked him to pray that he not be drafted into the army.

The rabbi asked, "Do you attend the house of prayer every morning?"

"No," he said, "I don't wake up till long after noon and then I go to play soccer."

"Are you keeping the Sabbath?" he asked.

"How can I? Saturday is reserved for the most important soccer games."

"Do you eat *kosher*?"

"It's cheaper to eat pork."

The rabbi persisted but he could not find a single point of merit to pray to G-d with. Finally, the rabbi said to him, "I envy you. Can you imagine? If you return to G-d out of love, you will become a greater rabbi than I."

"How is that possible?" he asked.

"You see, anyone who returns to G-d out of love has his sins turned into merits. You definitely have more sins than I have merits. In one minute, you can turn everything around and end up with more merits than me."

A reflective, thoughtful look came across this young man's face and he said, "Rabbi, wait another year and you will envy me even more."

Of course, then it would not work. When you love G-d, you are so overwhelmed with longing that you are ready to cast off everything that stands in the way. To the soccer player, the opportunity to indulge himself further in his own lifestyle was the overriding goal. Rabbi Elazar ben Durdaya, by comparison, realized that self-indulgence had ruined him. His love of G-d was so great, he was ready to forfeit all of his investment in the lifestyle which estranged him from G-d.

Imagine it this way: A top-ten-wanted-list criminal escapes into hiding. Among other measures, the police put a 24-hour a day surveillance net around his mother's house. After several years at large and out of contact with her, it suddenly strikes this criminal how sick his beloved mother must be over never being able to see her son again. He knows that if he steps anywhere near her he is going to get caught and put away for life, but his love for her is so great that he walks into the trap despite the consequences to himself. That was Elazar ben Durdaya.

His entire life, he immersed himself in his own immediate enjoyment. He was not afraid to lose his everlasting life; it didn't matter to him, it was too removed, etc. Then, finally, after realizing how his self-indulgence had isolated him so, he was able to think about others. The first 'other' he thought about was his Maker. It suddenly dawned on him how G-d must have felt. He reasoned something like the following: If G-d made creation without needing anything in return, then we must be no less than a child to Him; how much He must hope for us to mature one day and realize the investment of love He has in us.

Rabbi Elazar ben Durdaya attained a love for G-d where he ceased worrying about the consequences to himself. He thus came to regret his past, not for his own sake but for G-d's. That was love of G-d. He was not a one-second-old when he died. He was a ninety-year-old. He used one moment to turn around his entire life.

Now, imagine if he had another moment and further deepened his return to G-d out of love. He would have been a 180 year old; and if he had another moment after that he would have been a 270 year old; and so on. That is the idea of eternity. Eternity means that one grows forever in this fashion with each moment doubling, tripling, quadrupling, etc. There is no calculating the value of the experience. Every moment is converted like Elazar ben Durdaya converted his final moment.

King David said, 'My sin is constantly before me.'[56] He only sinned once, and yet he capitalized on that sin over and over again to return to G-d out of love. With every moment of reflection on his one shortcoming, he fabricated a new and better eternal world for himself.

What is a moment worth? If, in that moment, one can come to the level of understanding and love of G-d that Elazar ben Durdaya did, then it truly is priceless. This is the Torah sensitivity to the value of life. This is why the laws of the Torah itself are suspended if life can be extended even one moment. Conversely, this is why if you take away one moment of life, even from a person on his deathbed, you are a murderer. You didn't take away a moment. You took away a potential for an entire life.

CHAPTER 5

YOM SHEKULO SHABBOS

In conclusion, the Torah says that there are two facets of life: there is life that exists within the framework of time, and there is life which transcends time and becomes eternity. It is possible to convert this limited life into limitless life. The body dies, but it is possible to become a partner with G-d in eternity.

When Abraham died after 175 years of life, the Torah testifies that he literally "came with his days."[57] What does that mean? It means he did not lose one day — even the days he spent exploring all his era's types of idol worship. All of it was converted into eternity.

As his true descendants, a Jew has a unique relationship to time. Into our hands has been placed the opportunity to bring about eternity, to bring about the original purpose in creation.

The Zohar points out that the Torah's opening word, *beraishis,* can also be read *bara shis,* meaning "(G-d) created six." The Zohar explains that this is a reference to the fact that G-d created the physical world to exist for six thousand years. Just as there were six days of creation and a seventh day of rest, so, too, there are six thousand years of the world, as we know it, and the seven thousandth year will be its Sabbath. In other words, at the end of six thousand years, time-bound history will conclude, and life in a beyond-time, eternal state will begin.

Yom shekulo Shabbos, referring to that era — the era which is literally 'entirely Sabbath' — is the real desire of G-d. It is His original intention. G-d didn't want to create this world. He wanted to create an existence that is *yom shekulo Shabbos* — an existence which is the perfect harmonization of Torah and this physical world.

Who makes that harmonization? G-d's partners — those who can see beyond themselves, and beyond the sixty second moment. Those who truly live as the descendants of Abraham, Isaac and Jacob.

I once met two Israelis who were working in the Negev. They worked in the nuclear reactor facility. Thousands of engineers worked there under the tightest security. These two young men had been working there ten years. I asked them to tell me if it was true that the Israelis had made the nuclear bomb. It was before that information became public knowledge.

They were quiet and traded smiles with each other. I told them that they could trust me. I wouldn't leak it to the newspapers or to anyone.

Finally, they told me, "Do you think that we really know anything?"

I said, "Yes. After all, you have been working there as engineers for ten years now. I can't believe that you don't know anything."

Then they began to explain to me the conditions under which they worked. "Every morning each worker goes into a private booth. A window opens up, and we are handed a bunch of parts, as well as instructions on how to put them together. We read the instructions, put the parts together, and pass it onto the next window. We have no idea if this part is needed for a bicycle, a motorcycle, an airplane, or a bomb. Periodically, we work in different booths so that in the end nobody knows exactly what he is doing. And this is the way we have worked for years."

Then they admitted to me that obviously there was at least one thing they understood: "There must be something very serious going on," they said. "How do we know? First, because so much thought and effort are put into keeping things secretive. And second, every part we have to work on comes with a detailed set of instructions which we must follow exactly or be penalized."

I thought to myself, "This is a beautiful illustration of

life."

We work in a secretive assembly line. What are we accomplishing? We don't really know. All we know is that it is called *yom shekulo Shabbos* — when we get there, we will see it.

Next, every one of us has a booth and is handed some fragments. Do we know what they are for? No. So, too, we were born in the middle of such and such an era, in such and such a place, under such and such circumstances. Our understanding is limited, fragmented. Do we know exactly how we got here? Do we know exactly where we are going? Do we know what each day will bring? No. Every day brings new surprises.

As long as we are in our booths, though, how can we expect to know more? If we would know more we would have no free choice. Who would not do it? When the Messiah comes, all the gentiles will run to be Jews — however, then it will be too late. Once we see the entire picture, we lose free choice. Therefore, G-d put us in booths. Our understanding now has to be limited.

Of course, even though we are in our booths there is one thing we know, and there is one thing which should settle us: Whatever surprises are handed us through the window, we can be sure there is an accompanying page of instructions. Under this condition act as follows; under another condition, do this. For instance, sometimes we get up in the morning and, G-d forbid, someone is sick, or there is some other unsettling news — our tendency is to feel overwhelmed. However, with each surprise comes the instruction page. The Torah tells us how to react. If we follow the instructions, we become a partner in the construction of *yom shekulo Shabbos,* we become a partner in eternity.

Of course, since our daily chores and responsibilities can seem tedious, fragmented and not fully meaningful, G-d also supplied us with the blueprint which can help us get a taste and a glimpse of what we are accomplishing. Torah is the blueprint. It connects us to the past and teaches us how to build the future. Nevertheless, its most important feature is that it brings us into the present.

Let me explain this.

I often get calls from people who are depressed. Almost invariably, their depression boils down to one of two things: either they are dwelling excessively on the past or fantasizing excessively about the future. They have no present. Or, to put it more accurately, they don't believe they have a present.

Living in the past or living in the future produces a spiritual and emotional numbness to the present. And a depressed person chooses that numbness over facing the pain of the present. They usually fail to realize that living with that numbness is what deepens their depression.

If I were to ask them: What is the opposite of pleasure? they will probably answer: pain. Pain, I tell them, is not the opposite of pleasure. Numbness, insensitivity, the inability to feel is the opposite of pleasure. However, because you believe that pain is the opposite of pleasure, you avoid it at all costs, despite the fact that the thing you should really be avoiding is numbness.

Life has pain. We all have to deal with pain. A depressed person thinks he is freed from the pain and failure that even the most successful people constantly deal with. If you don't feel the pain, then you won't feel the pleasure either. You should welcome the pain, I tell them. It means that you are alive. Without the pain there is no pleasure. Your whole problem, though, is that you try to numb out the moment; you opt to hide in the womb of the past or the tomb of the future rather than facing the present ready to be born.

The Torah's primary value to us is not its historical value and not it predictive glimpse into the future world. The Torah tells us about the moment. It tells us how to live now . . . this moment we are all part of.

Is keeping it hard? Is there pain? Yes. And isn't that fantastic? Isn't the pain wonderful? It means we are alive. It means we can feel the pleasure. So, the next time you see a non-Torah person living 'happily ever after' in his comfortable numbness, remember to cry a tear for him. He is not even alive yet. Take a deep breath and thank G-d that you are alive.

Thank you and good night.

After the lecture, a group of people gathered around the rabbi to ask questions. Ruth and David, too, were part of the group. They waited, and when their turn came, they expressed their thanks to the rabbi and asked a few quick questions. Seeing that it was getting late, they finished up and wished him farewell.

The lecture hall was almost empty now and on his way out David glanced over his shoulder. He noticed that the young man he had sat next to, and who before the lecture had been asking him questions, had stepped forward and was standing alone with the rabbi. A memory flashed in front of David. That person was him a couple of years ago. All of a sudden, it struck David how much he had grown. A chill went down his spine. And as the momentary sensation passed, two words came to his lips, *"Boruch Hashem."*

ROSH HASHANNAH
Unveiling The Purpose of Creation

The essay on *Rosh HaShannah* is adapted from tape #1039, which was delivered in the month of Elul 5750 (September 1990). Although not connected to the dialogue aspect of *Choose Life!,* the underlying theme is the same: The Purpose of Creation. It should not be necessary, then, to have read the book till this point in order to understand the contents of this essay.

ROSH HASHANNAH
Unveiling The Purpose Of Creation

Every *Yom Tov* is designed to give us something — to leave deposited in us a perceptively tangible by-product (of attitude or being) once it passes.

For instance, *Pesach* (Passover) gives us *yetzias mitzraim*, literally the exodus from Egypt. More than the physical oppression, Egypt represented a state of mind typified by Pharaoh, who in turn represented the philosophy, "Power and might are determined by my hand" (or in the modern idiom, "Might makes right"). *Pesach,* therefore, gives us *yetzias mitzraim,* the ability to unfetter ourselves from the spiritual shackles of this mentality.

The *Yom Tov* of *Shavuos* gives us *kabalas haTorah,* receiving of the Torah. The greater use we make of *Shavuos,* the more Torah it helps us produce. *Yom Kippur* gives us *mechilas avonos,* the ability to have our sins forgiven and become cleansed of the spiritual soot which accumulated over the year. *Succos,* sitting under the protective roof of the *Shechinah* (the Divine Presence), gives us the opportunity to experience a unique, intimate closeness to G-d. *Chanukah* gives us the light — the secrets — of Torah. *Purim* gives us the ability to wipe out the memory of Amalek, the representative of unadulterated evil.

What does *Rosh HaShannah* give us? Think about the answer before reading on.

Rosh HaShannah

Rosh HaShannah is unique because it is not what it gives us which matters, but rather what we give it. This needs explanation.

The end goal of creation is that G-d should become king: "And then G-d will be King over all the world" we say in our *Rosh HaShannah* prayers. *Rosh HaShannah* is the time to coronate G-d king, to be *mamlich HaKodesh Boruch Hu.* "Say in front of Me *malchios* (i.e., verses of kingship) in order to make Me king over you."

Why does G-d ask us to make Him king?

Of course, G-d is not an entity we can project human frailty and egoism onto; He does not need to become king for His sake. What, then, is the underlying principle in crowning Him king?

G-d, by definition, can do everything and anything. However, He created the world in such a way that He "cannot" attain the one thing He wants without first receiving the input of man, and that is: G-d "cannot" make Himself a king.

The term "king" has lost much of its intended meaning

for us nowadays. A king is not a dictator. True, dictators subjugate nations and peoples, however, they are not kings because the people do not willfully and longingly accept their rulership. Saddam Hussein is not king of Kuwait because his army overran and imposed its laws on that country. A king, in the original sense of the word, is a ruler who is accepted by his subjects. "There is no king without subjects."[58]

Since G-d desired to create man with free will, He, at one and the same time, infused the world with the presence of His majesty and yet created (to a degree) the appearance that the forces of nature run independently of His rule. This simultaneously hidden yet manifest majesty allows man to exercise free will; it gives him the choice to penetrate beneath the surface and perceive the majesty or remain deceived by surface appearances.

Only through the free will of the subjects can the ruler be crowned king in the true sense of the word. Therefore, G-d created the world in such a way that He, so to speak, waits eagerly for man, who has been bestowed with free will, to crown him king.

Therefore, *Rosh HaShannah* is a unique *Yom Tov* because in essence the orientation is not: What do we get out of it? but rather: What do we give it? What do we give G-d?

And what is it that we give G-d on *Rosh HaShannah*? Kingship.

Of course, it is true that in giving G-d kingship, we get as much if not more than any act of receiving. After all, the Husseins and the totalitarian governments, the crumbling parliamentary democracies, and the self-serving politicians all accentuate for us how much *we* need to crown G-d king. Similarly, on the individual level, self-styled psychologists, media gurus, and even the best laid plans of our own minds drive home to us how limited we are to affect our own good. History — global and personal — proves that man cannot successfully rule himself. Only when he submits himself to the rule and will of the Creator, can he hope to free his spirit. There is no king but Him, and no one but we benefit by living under His benevolent, fatherly direction.

What exactly does it mean to give G-d kingship, to coronate Him?

It means to acknowledge His overwhelming presence in our lives. And to do so with a depth and understanding that ultimately translates into changed and renewed actions. It means making G-d's will our will.

This is by no means an easy task. Ignorance, laziness, physical desires, and ego often prevent us from seeing or performing what is ultimately best for us. Therefore, G-d blessed us with a day devoted exclusively to this service: *Rosh HaShannah.*

Of course, it is a year-round job. *Rosh HaShannah* is merely the time when coronating G-d is emphasized, with the understanding and expectation that it will energize us to coronate Him in all our activities for the remainder of the year. However, this one day is an especially opportune time for all of us to join as one and focus on giving G-d the one thing He 'needs' us to give Him: our free-willed allegiance to His kingship.

Crowning G-d for all Humanity

Every individual is responsible to crown G-d king in his or her own life. Among all of mankind, however, G-d chose one people to act as His representatives, to lead the way. That people, of course, is *om Yisroel*, the people of Israel. G-d has charged *om Yisroel* specifically with the task of coronating Him king for the whole world to see, and eventually follow.

Only once in history did all of humanity accept G-d as a king. Think about it for a second. When was that time?

It was not *matan Torah*, the revelation at Mount Sinai, because the gentiles (excluding Yisro, Moshe's father-in-law) did not accept it. It was not even during Noah's time, because in the ark with him was his son Cham (Ham). The only time when all humanity accepted G-d as king was in the time of Adam, before he had children. All humanity existed in this one person, and that one person knew G-d in His entirety.

Adam was created with the ability to fully recognize G-d. The *Talmud* says that he saw from one end of the world to the other, which means that wherever he looked, he saw *malchus Hashem*, the kingship of G-d.

However, for the purposes of free will, he was created with the potential for his vision to become askewed. He had within him the potential to deny G-d. And since Adam was given the entire world, if he would have recognized G-d as king, automatically the entire world would have recognized G-d as king.

Of course, Adam sinned and lost his vantage point; he no longer saw everything clearly. In fact, his own son Cain rebelled against G-d. His grandson Enosh in fact is credited with inventing idol worship.[59]

In those early days of creation, only Noah was able to remain righteous. Even Noah's accomplishments, however, were limited in comparison to Abraham, who became the father of the nation Israel. What was the difference between Abraham and Noah?

Noah attained the heights of righteousness in the man-to-G-d relationship. Nevertheless, he lacked (compared to Abraham) in his concern over G-d's investment, namely — creation, mankind; he was not the equal of Abraham in the man-to-man relationship.

This difference is illustrated in the way each stood up to the opposition in his time. In Noah's time, Enosh had caused his generation to totally deny G-d. Although Noah is credited with maintaining his righteousness in the face of all opposition, yet he did not win over the opposition to his side, to the side of G-d. As a result, the world was destroyed.

In Abraham's time, Nimrod rose to power. Nimrod

had incited the entire world to unite and converge on Babylon (modern day Iraq) with the express purpose of building the ultimate monument of defiance to G-d: the Tower of Babel. And he was successful. He had declared himself god, and all of humanity was united in agreement over his rulership, including Abraham's very father.

(As an aside, it is interesting to note that today many people and nations talk about the world uniting as one. However, the lesson of the Tower of Babel is that unity, in and of itself, is not an absolutely good value. If the purpose of unity is to seek to wipe out the rulership of G-d, as was the intention of Nimrod, then it is bad.)

The era of Nimrod's ascension to power marked the antithesis of the world before Adam sinned. Adam, the height of creation, saw G-d in His full majesty; Nimrod, one of the lowest human beings ever to live, declared himself a man-god, and convinced the entire world to accept his dominion.

Nimrod, however, represented the kernel of Adam's sin blown up to its full proportions. When Adam sinned, he hid himself.[60] This showed that he had lost his full clarity of vision; it reflected his perception that a place existed where G-d could not find him, where G-d's rule did not extend. Similarly, when the entire world accepted the man-god, self-declared king Nimrod, it was their way of saying they preferred a king with human limits who could not possibly know everything they did, and who would therefore not intrude in their lives too much, i.e., someone who would let them hide.

Into this milieu stepped Abraham. When he came to the conclusion on his own that G-d was the only true king, he was immediately ready to sacrifice his life in order to advertise the truth. His love of G-d drove him to do that which G-d "could not": teach and persuade others to coronate Him king. This was the level of love and total self-sacrifice that Noah did not reach.

Thus, perhaps the most telling incident in Abraham's life was when he was 99-years-old. While recovering from his circumcision, G-d suddenly appeared before him (by no means an everyday experience even for an Abraham). In the midst of this experience, which would seem to be the very goal and height of an individual's purpose for living, three strangers appeared in the distance. Abraham broke communication with G-d in order to show hospitality to these passers-by, whom to Abraham appeared as idol-worshipping Arabs (even though, as revealed later, they were angels).[61]

How could Abraham do such a thing, ceasing a revelation of G-d in order to feed a few undignified strangers? The *Talmud* tells us, however, that we learn a central lesson from this Abraham's behavior. We learn that in this world kindness to others takes precedence even over receiving the Divine Presence.[62]

What led Abraham to act the way he did? How did he know to do this?

The answer is his love of G-d. Because he loved G-d

so much, even the personal high of experiencing G-d face to face was secondary to protecting G-d's interests in this world: namely, that all humanity should come to recognize Him as king, even — and especially — those people furthest away.

The Rambam wrote:[63] Abraham went out, travelled all over, met with thousands and thousands of people, and taught them "each according to his own capacity." In other words, no person was below Abraham's dignity. He spoke with young and old, criminals and nobility, simpletons and intellectuals — all in ways they were accustomed to. He had one mission: to restore the dignity of G-d, to teach the entire world about the grandeur and majesty of the Creator. And for that his own dignity was secondary.

Abraham's love of G-d was greater than Noah's because his love inspired him to change the world in the face of all odds. *Chazal*, the Sages, tell us that Abraham was called *HaIvri* (the Hebrew) because he stood on one "side" (*eyver*, the Hebrew word related to *Ivri*, means 'side') while the entire world stood on the other.[64] Ideologically, he opposed everything his contemporaries found sacred.

Abraham was willing to sacrifice everything to succeed in his mission. His single-minded dedication reached the point where he smashed his father's idols, was tried in public, threatened with death, and brought before Nimrod, where he told the self-proclaimed god to his face that he was a fraud, a nothing. Nimrod responded with threats to throw Abraham into a furnace. Abraham, who knew not to rely on a miracle, did not expect one. All he knew was that G-d's honor was at stake; consequently he considered it a privilege to let himself be thrown into the fire and give up his life.

Of course, G-d did save him, and as a result the ministers in power deposed Nimrod. (It is interesting to note that they did not accept Abraham's contentions concerning a benevolent, all-knowing Creator, but instead merely got rid of Nimrod, rationalizing that he was an inadequate representative of their philosophy of defiance of G-d, and a poor spokesman for their assertion that man makes a better king over himself than G-d.)

Chazal tell us that after this sequence of events, Nimrod became lost and was on the verge of starving to death. All of a sudden he saw a tent: it was the tent of Abraham, which was well-known as a sanctuary open to all strangers and vagabonds who sought food and shelter. Swallowing his pride, he allowed Abraham to nurse him back to health. As was Abraham's custom, the only fee he required of his guests upon their departure was a simple blessing acknowledging G-d as the source of all the food and good. Nimrod could not even bring himself to do that, and preferred instead to offer himself as a servant to Abraham.

What is the message here? Truth, in the end, wins out.

It even comes to acquire that which falsehood so desperately sought to possess. Nimrod, the one-time ruler of all humanity, became a servant to the man who stubbornly opposed him and clung to the truth. While Nimrod sank lower and lower, Abraham soared higher and higher — they eventually reversed positions until Abraham became world renowned and was crowned by G-d as "the father of a multitude of nations."

Abraham wanted to restore the world to its original state where all humanity recognized G-d as king. That idea fueled everything he did. As a result, G-d made him father of the nation whose purpose is to crown G-d king for all of humanity, whose entire existence is for fulfilling the one thing G-d "cannot" do for Himself: being *mamlich HaKodesh Boruch Hu*, coronating G-d. There is no king without subjects. It is *om Yisroel* who make G-d king.

The Power of *Kiddush Hashem*

In truth, every place should be completely filled with G-d's presence. G-d is everything, every place, every time. Therefore, He should not need anyone to make Him king.

For the purposes of creation, however, a thing, a place, a time had to be hollowed out of this objective reality called G-d. The world is that place. It is a constriction of G-dliness; a place where G-d is somewhat removed and hidden. That is why the Hebrew word for world is *olam,* which also means hidden.[65]

This world then is a *chalal,* literally a "hollow," where the full brilliance of G-d's presence is constricted. The *chalal,* however, can be filled, and man was put in this world to do just that. Wherever and whenever man fills the *chalal,* he produces *kiddush Hashem,* the sanctification of G-d. Wherever and whenever he fails to do so, the result is *chilul* (a variant of *chalal*) *Hashem,* a desecration of G-d.

Thus, man has been blessed to "fill the earth and conquer her."[66] On a deeper level, it means that he must fill the physical, material world with *kiddush Hashem* and conquer it so that no place remains devoid of G-dliness. Therefore, *kiddush Hashem* and coronating G-d are one and the same idea. Wherever we conduct ourselves according to the will of G-d — wherever we coronate G-d — we make *kiddush Hashem.*

The Rambam writes that any righteous act performed when nobody else is looking is a *kiddush Hashem.*[67] In other words, he dispels the misconception that *kiddush Hashem* entails only public sanctification of G-d. The essential idea behind sanctifying G-d is performing His will under even the most difficult circumstances. Private acts, in some ways, produce the most far-reaching sanctifications of G-d.

Why is a private act so difficult? Because people are naturally predisposed to doing things based on what others will think of them; and if they do good things in public it is usually the desire for public recognition which brought them to do it.

Actions performed in private, on the other hand, are often the barometer of greatness because they are performed exclusively from the person's own internal conscience. Ultimately, private acts prove that the person had G-d in mind, and only G-d in mind; they, therefore, affirm G-d's existence in a uniquely powerful way.

A person, for instance, can perform a great *kiddush Hashem* when he is walking down the street and comes upon a newsstand displaying unbecoming images. Although no one else would know one way or the other, he averts his eyes. That affirms the recognition that G-d is operating in his life; that is a *kiddush Hashem* even though no one knows about it. Saying blessings over food with care and concentration, accepting hardship with a genuine love, etc. are also forms of *kiddush Hashem*.

Kiddush Hashem, therefore, comes in two basic forms: public and private. Its quality is gauged by the degree of difficulty involved in maintaining allegiance to the will of G-d. *Kiddush Hashem* also has another important aspect: the after-effects are not necessarily immediately seen or easy to understand. It is like planting a seed, the results of which are not seen until later. This delay, this distancing of cause and effect, adds to the difficulty of maintaining allegiance to G-d's will.

There is an awe-inspiring story of the Holocaust about a Jew who had managed to survive the worst the concentration camps had to offer. Two hours before the Allied soldiers were to liberate the camp, the Nazi commandant convened the Jews. He singled out this one man and told him, "For five years you have survived the camps and never once did you eat non-*kosher* food. I know that you have risked so much just to keep the smallest details of your religion. However, you were willing to take the risk because you knew you were going to die; your life meant nothing to you. Now, however, you will be freed in two hours. Let's see how much your religion is really worth to you. Here is some pork. Eat it now or I will kill you right here."

Excluding the three cardinal sins of murder, adultery and idolatry, a Jew is commanded to transgress the Torah to save his life. However, when the oppressor's intention is explicitly to get the Jew to deny the Torah, then even if he tells him to change the color of his shoelaces, the Jew must be prepared to give up his life.

So it was with this Jew in the camps. He refused the pork sandwich and was killed for doing so.

Later, when the Jew's daughter found out that her father had forfeited his life just two hours before liberation because he refused to eat pork her grief was compounded beyond her capacity to bear. Upon settling in the land of Israel, she became irreligious and raised her children to be irreligious like her.

One of the ways this woman tried to indoctrinate her children was by sending them into Tel-Aviv to buy pork.

Her son, a fully secularized, non-religious Israeli, was on line to buy pork one day when something strange happened. Waiting on line, pushing for a better position, all of a sudden the story of his grandfather came to his mind. He stood there thinking, "How can I be here on a line pushing to buy the very food for which my grandfather gave up his life in order not to eat it?"

The young man got off the line, and decided then and there never to eat anything non-*kosher* again. Some time later he decided to keep *Shabbos*. Eventually, he decided to start learning Torah. He excelled at his studies, and now heads one of the most influential organizations for turning unaffiliated Jews back to Judaism.

To the Nazis who saw this Jew's grandfather die because he refused to compromise his religion, the *kiddush Hashem* was immediate. However, to some Jews the effect was not only not immediate, but was even seen as a *chilul Hashem*. Only years later, now, can we look back and see clearly how that Jew's grandfather's action constituted one of the highest acts of *kiddush Hashem;* and that indeed his very action is the direct cause of a renewed allegiance to G-d and Judaism of many, many of today's Jews.

The purpose of life is to generate *kiddush Hashem,* acknowledging His kingship through the unique, individual circumstances of our public and private lives. Often that entails great difficulty — but that is precisely the point. An easy life is not necessarily a successful or good life; a meaningful life is one where the person finds within himself or herself the strength and courage to withstand short-term, seemingly negative after-effects for the sake of carrying out G-d's will. And whether it is now or later, apparent or not, every act of allegiance to the kingship of G-d is a *kiddush Hashem* which cuts across time and space and has a monumental effect on the running of the universe, on the very purpose of creation.

The Generator of Light

Kiddush Hashem is like a generator. You are probably reading this in a well-lit room. Where is the light coming from? From a generator operated by the local utility company. The generator is not seen; it is far away, inside a building, encased in machinery, yet it is producing the power to light not only this room but hundreds of thousands of other rooms.

Fulfilling our inward duties to G-d — loving Him for the pain (which is always corrective whether we see it or not) as well as for the good, performing His will when we are the only one who seems to know it is right, etc. — produces a power beyond our comprehension. All of a sudden, an alienated Jew on a college campus in Texas wakes up one morning and decides to try out a weekend at a Torah retreat.

Where did he get that inspiration from? From the *kiddush Hashem* performed in the private lives of people like you and me. Where did an alienated, secular Israeli pushing on line to buy pork, get the inspiration to get off the line, change his life, and become a force in the movement to return Jews to their heritage? From the power of his grandfather's *kiddush Hashem*, which itself was generated by the voltage first produced by his great-grandparents, which itself is ultimately rooted in the kilowatts of *kiddush Hashem* first produced by the actions of Abraham.

Abraham's life was one unrelenting test after another. The purpose of his tests was to give him the opportunity to coronate G-d in the most difficult circumstances in order to produce and maximize the wattage output of his *kiddush Hashem* for future generations.

Therefore, G-d tested Abraham numerous times: at Nimrod's furnace; when he was told, *lech-lecha*, to completely abandon his father's house and land; when his wife was taken before him, which occurred twice; when he was told to bring his only son as a sacrifice, etc. — G-d tested him from all possible angles, and yet he never complained. His awareness that G-d was present as king even through the worst times, never waned. The ultimate goal of these tests were to infuse forever into his seed the ability to overcome the situations which he himself overcame.

The Chasam Sofer asked: Where have the Jewish people acquired their resiliency to withstand persecution — including unequaled inquisitions, pogroms and holocausts — only to be exiled from those same inhospitable countries, and yet rebuild, start anew, and rise to prominence in a new country almost overnight?

By rights, the Jewish people should have vanished like every other vanquished and persecuted population. However, we have defied the laws of history (which should otherwise be no less absolute than the law of gravity, for instance), the Chasam Sofer writes, because of the power of Abraham, who was told to abandon his birthplace and father's house and venture forth penniless into the unknown. He earned the right to have transmitted to his seed this supernatural resiliency because he withstood the test of abandoning the security of his own home and country.

With each test, Abraham became greater, and the light he spread more brilliant. By nurturing and bringing to full fruition the ability to coronate G-d in even the darkest of circumstances, Abraham permanently instilled into his children the same potential. Thus, we from the seed of Abraham, also have concealed within us a unique potential to turn darkness into light.

This, then, is the dynamic operating behind the suffering of the Jewish people. Suffering is a darkness; it is a fact of existence which contradicts the existence of G-d. Nevertheless, it exists in G-d's world because the original hiddenness (necessary for creation and free will) was increased dramatically by man, starting with Adam down through Nimrod and Hitler.

The *om Yisroel*, as the children of Abraham, Isaac and

Israel, have been sent out on a mission to coronate G-d wherever His rule is denied, wherever darkness now reigns. Israel suffers more than any other nation or people because our mission is to enter the thick darkness of *chilul Hashem* and turn it into the brilliant light of *kiddush Hashem.*

This is the power Abraham infused his seed with: the power to pull out of the pitch blackness a thread of light, and turn that light into a flood of brilliant illumination. The more dark and hollowed out a place is, the more brilliant the light when *kiddush Hashem* is accomplished. *Kiddush Hashem* and coronating G-d are one and the same idea. Wherever we conduct ourselves according to the will of G-d — wherever we coronate G-d — we make *kiddush Hashem*, we fill the *chalal.*

Kiddush Hashem Is Never Withheld

In the concentration camps, G-d took away *Shabbos* from us; He took away *kosher* food, family life — the one thing He did not take away was the ability to coronate Him king — *kiddush Hashem*, sanctifying G-d. On the contrary, the potential for *kiddush Hashem* was raised to never-before-reached heights because of the deep concealment of His presence.

When *Yom Kippur* came and a Jew had to eat some food to save his life (as the Torah commands him to do in that situation) — and from that meal he was able to live a little longer and join nine other men to answer the

'kaddish' prayer: *Amen, yehay shmay rabah mivorach . . .*
— his very eating on *Yom Kippur* was a *kiddush Hashem*!

As we said, *kiddush Hashem* does not only entail literally giving up one's life, and it is not only for concentration camps. Every Jew has a different assignment concerning where to make G-d king: the businessman in the business world, the *yeshiva*-man in the *yeshiva* world; the career woman in her career, and the housewife in the house; the parents without children and the couple with more children than they can handle; the wealthy person and the poor; the healthy and the sick; the young and the old — no one is ever at any time withheld from coronating G-d, because that is the bottom line of everyone's existence in this world.

Nevertheless, it is one thing to coronate G-d when everything goes well. It is another thing to coronate G-d in Auschwitz or Treblinka. It is one thing to coronate G-d when your family is healthy, business goes well, and you have time to learn Torah. It is another thing to coronate G-d when a person is, G-d forbid, childless or, G-d forbid, sick, or, G-d forbid, without an income.

In the *Rosh HaShannah* prayers we say, "Your glory should reign over the entire world — all of it" (*kaul haolam kulo*). Why the extra word *kulo*, "all of it"? The meaning is: You should be recognized as and declared king whether in the Holy of Holies of the Holy Temple or in the gas chambers of Auschwitz; in the happiest situation or the saddest situation You should be king.

Making a *kiddush Hashem* when everything is going well is by no means easy or demeaning; it is, however, only one type of *kiddush Hashem*; and it is a *kiddush Hashem* where G-d gives us most of the means we need to sanctify Him. However, in the camps, where everything was taken away, the *kiddush Hashem* was disproportionately based on the individual's effort.

The Torah Readings for *Rosh HaShannah*

The difference between a *kiddush Hashem* supported mostly by G-d versus one where G-d's input is hardly seen at all is actually the difference between Torah readings prescribed for both days of *Rosh HaShannah*. On the first day, we read about the birth of Isaac, *leidas* Yitzchak. On the second day, we read about the binding of Isaac, *akeidas* Yitzchak. Both recount wonderful examples of *kiddush Hashem*.

In the first day's reading we are reminded how an elderly couple, Sarah 90-years-old and Abraham 100-years-old — a childless couple whom most outsiders would have pitied for their outwardly unrewarded devotion to an invisible G-d — had their years of devotion rewarded with a child. Think of what a great impression, what a great *kiddush Hashem*, that made in the eyes of humanity.

On the second day of *Rosh HaShannah*, we read about the binding of Yitzchak (Isaac). After Abraham and Sarah finally gave birth to the child they yearned for so desperately, G-d told Abraham to give him back. Abraham not only complied but did so with a full heart, because he was able to distinguish in his mind between his own needs and the needs of G-d. G-d needs allegiance to His will, *kiddush Hashem,* and if His will is to sacrifice Yitzchak, then Abraham could completely forgo his personal needs for the sake of G-d.

Now, which *kiddush Hashem* had a greater impact on humanity: *leidas* Yitzchak (the birth of Isaac) or *akeidas* Yitzchak (the binding of Isaac [on the altar])? Superficially, it would appear that this devoted couple being rewarded with a son after so many years is a greater sanctification of G-d. After all, it was a miracle for all to see — a clear-cut proof of G-d's limitless power. The *akeidas* Yitzchak was a great personal feat, for sure, but it was a basically private act measured by only internal standards.

The truth is, however, that *akeidas* Yitzchak was greater. Open miracles are sanctifications of G-d which require only minimal human input. A *kiddush Hashem* like *akeidas* Yitzchak allows for much greater human input — Abraham became a full-fledged partner in bringing about this sanctification. Listening to G-d went against all logic; he was losing everything and gaining nothing. Nevertheless, it was exactly this concealment of G-d which produced the greater *kiddush Hashem* of *akeidas* Yitzchak.

Nimrod's inferno and Hitler's inferno were one and

the same: they were places of the seemingly complete obscurity of G-d's presence. Yet, like their forefather Abraham, many, many Jews coronated G-d king even in the camps and serenely walked into the gas chamber (to the disbelief of the Nazis), with *Shma Yisroel Hashem Elokeinu Hashem Echad,* "Hear O'Israel, G-d is our G-d, G-d is One" on their lips.[68]

G-d performed a miracle for Abraham and saved him from Nimrod's furnace. However, that was ultimately G-d's *kiddush Hashem*. If G-d would raise all six million from the ashes, the entire world would acknowledge Him as Master and king. But that would be G-d's doing. It would be, *lehavdil*, like a dictator imposing his will on his subjects. There would be no free choice on our part to deny his kingship.

When we, the survivors, continue to serve G-d with absolute devotion and love, we produce our own *kiddush Hashem*, a *kiddush Hashem* based greatly on our own input. By doing so, we, in fact, sanctify the lives of the six million who perished, and produce a light very little else can conceivably match.

Biyas haMoshiach

Abraham's house was open to everyone. As mentioned above, he only requested one thing of them in return for his hospitality: a simple blessing. Why was he satisfied with teaching his guests to recite a blessing?

The verse says, "What does G-d *request* of you

. . . only that you fear Him." The *Talmud* comments on the verse as follows: Don't read "What (*mah*) does G-d request . . . ?" Read "One hundred (*meah*) G-d requests of you." In other words, the *Talmud* concludes, this is where we learn that G-d "requests" from us one hundred blessings every day.[69]

Usually one makes a 'request' of another if he cannot perform or attain the object of the request on his own. G-d 'requests' blessings from us. Why? Because a blessing is a miniature coronation. "Blessed are you G-d, *King* of the universe . . ." we utter many times a day. G-d "cannot" make us make Him king, therefore, He only "requests" that we do so. Each blessing is an opportunity beckoning us to coronate G-d.

We can coronate G-d under all circumstances, whether tangibly and openly or whether sitting alone in a room through uttering a blessing over a glass of water: "Blessed are You G-d, King of the universe . . . ." Saying blessings or saying '*Boruch Hashem,*' even during sad and tragic times, is a recognition of G-d's existence which only you and He truly appreciate. It reflects a genuine personal closeness between creation and Creator.

This type of behavior makes G-d king and brings *Moshiach.* How? *Rosh HaShannah* is actually a miniature *biyas haMoshiach*, a microcosm of the coming of the Messiah, because just as it is a day to coronate G-d, so, too, when *Moshiach* comes, "then the G-d will be king over the entire world."

When that day arrives, the world will ask: Who made G-d king? The answer of course is: every Jew, starting from Abraham. And at that awesome time everyone will be able to recognize his part in the bringing about of this great day for mankind.

Ironically, no doubt all of us will be shocked and dismayed about the part we played in making G-d king. Things which we thought were high points may turn out to be virtually insignificant; and the things most unappreciated by mankind (ourselves included) — those secret, private acts — will take on earth-shaking proportions.

Rosh HaShannah is called the "day of covering" because it is the only *Yom Tov* which coincides with the new moon, the lunar phase when the moon is entirely covered except for the first sliver of light around its perimeter. To those who walk in darkness the moon's darkness can be viewed as an ominous sign. However, the truth is just the opposite; the darkness is nothing but a precursor to the light. And to those who dedicate their lives to generating the light of *kiddush Hashem* — and who see in the "day of covering" the opportunity to recharge their own generators of light — then the sparkle of redemption is just over the horizon.

Appendix

BACK TO THE FUTURE
Breaking Codes Through Mathematical Sequences[*]

By S. Ornstein

Harold Gans, a senior mathematician with the U.S. Department of Defense, sat at his home computer and squinted as he tapped in the last of the data. The die was cast. The results that would emerge from the next 19 days and nights of computer processing — with the PC humming away while Gans slept, while he breakfasted with his wife, while he commuted to his job at the defense department — would confirm or deny the novel experiments taking place at a university 7,000 miles away in the Jerusalem hills.

Gans was searching for G-d through mathematical sequences.

A religious Jew who had studied Hebrew texts since he was a small boy, the now 45-year-old Gans never anticipated that it would be his secular background — specifically, his knowledge of math and statistics — which would draw him into the most controversial and fascinating religious research

---

[*]   Originally published in *Lifestyles* (a Canadian publication) and reprinted here with permission from the author.

of recent years.

What Gans and a few scholarly counterparts in Jerusalem were researching was a system of intricate codes found in the Hebrew letters of the Five Books of Moses. The codes, embedded as single letters spaced at even intervals throughout the Hebrew text (for example, every 50th letter) form words, phrases and sentences that, researchers say, provide detailed information about human history up to the present day.

Woven like an intricate tapestry through the 3,300-year-old text, with chains of meaning running backwards and forwards, the codes form such intriguing, complex designs that they seem to defy the possibility of coincidence.

But it is their ability to predict the future — to predict events that have taken place as recently as the 1981 assassination of Egyptian President Anwar Sadat, including the name of the chief assassin, the date, Sadat's name and the Hebrew words for "president," "shot," "gunfire," "murder" and "parade" (Sadat was shot and killed during a parade) in a single passage — that has given researchers and others who have come in contact with the codes cause to rethink the prevailing post-modern view that questions the divinity of the Torah, and places it among other works by human authors.

The new research represents a daring return to the ancient Jewish tradition which maintains that this is not an ordinary text written by ordinary men, but rather, a communication by an all-knowing Being — a Being who was concerned not only with communicating broad philosophical precepts, but who gave the utmost care to each letter of the text, again paralleling the age-old story of G-d dictating the text to Moses on Mount Sinai, letter by letter.

Mathematicians, like Professor Kazhdan of Harvard, who have reviewed the codes research, say it's rigorous and impressive.

Kazhdan and colleagues from the mathematics department of Harvard, Yale and the Hebrew University in Jerusalem called the work "serious research carried out by serious investigators" in the letter of approbation they wrote for the preface of *Maymad HaNosaf (The Added Dimension)*, a recent book by chief codes researcher Professor Doron Witztum of the Jerusalem College of Technology. Acknowledging that the ramifications of the research are potentially extremely controversial, the reviewers said, "The results obtained are sufficiently striking to deserve a wide audience," and they urged further research.

Years ago, Gans had dismissed the idea of codes embedded in the Torah as "ridiculous."

"It sounded so off-the-wall to me," he said. "I disbelieved it immediately."

But relatives persuaded the doubting mathematician to attend a Staten Island seminar on the codes. Gans brought along a friend, Dr. Andrew Goldfinger, senior physicist at the Johns Hopkins University Applied Physics Laboratory.

At the event, the Israeli presenter displayed codes that dazzled the audience. From a Book of Genesis passage, he pointed out a cluster of encoded words detailing the French Revolution: "Mapecha HaSarfatit" (Hebrew for "the French Revolution"), "Louie," "Beit" (House of) "Bourbon," "HaMarseilles" (the French anthem) and "Bastilla," the French political prison. The biblical passage in question describes the imprisonment of the patriarch Joseph in Egypt. The word "Bastilla" is encoded across a sentence of the

Hebrew text which reads "the prison in which the king keeps his prisoners."

Although Gans and Goldfinger intuitively felt the codes might be significant, as scientists they were dissatisfied by the scientific back-up. They expected something meatier — experiments with rigorous controls, for example.

But their skepticism began to falter when the speaker displayed the results of an extremely complex codes experiment — one perhaps only scientists could love.

Researcher Witztum had done a correlation study on the Book of Genesis which revealed that the names of dozens of great rabbis in Jewish history were repeatedly found encoded very close to their yahrtzeits, the anniversary dates of their deaths. Again and again, the experiment showed the pairs (rabbi and yahrtzeit) would appear inexplicably close, as if drawn together by a magnetic force.

Witztum had crafted the experiment to minimize human interference in the results. The rabbis were chosen by a set criterion: They were the ones whose biographies took up more than three columns of text in a Hebrew encyclopedia.

The chance that the phenomenon was occurring at random was extraordinarily small: one in 775 million.

Gans and Goldfinger nodded to each other in silent approval of the experiment. The math checked out, this was it. The off-the-wall was becoming believable.

A few months later, Gans attended a second presentation of the codes, this time in his hometown of Baltimore, at the Sheraton Inner Harbor Hotel. Aish HaTorah, a Jewish outreach organization with branches in Jerusalem and around the world, was presenting codes as part of its Discovery

Seminar. Created in Israel by a team of scientists, mathematicians and Judaic Scholars called Arachim, and then adapted to English by Aish HaTorah, the seminar is designed to show the depth and validity of the Torah and the Jewish way of life.

In the seminar audience that evening was Michael Epstein, 45, a real estate developer and manufacturer who was sitting in on his third Discovery seminar. A non-religious Jew and a prominent member of the Republican lobby group, The National Jewish Coalition, Epstein had first seen the seminar in Washington, D.C. a year earlier and was shocked and unraveled by the computer presentation.

"It hit me in the mouth," he said, "I was able to explain away everything else, or just not pay attention."

The seminar upset his formerly firm conviction that the Torah was written by men. "How could men have done it? It was impressive enough for men to have written the Torah. But to write Torah and codes . . ."

Although Epstein couldn't find any mistakes in the presentation, he was so jarred that he remained very skeptical. He suspected he was being duped.

"I went a second time," he said, "and I brought as many friends as I could twist arms, to help me find out where they'd tricked me." But again, none of them could find holes in the logic.

Now, at his third Discovery Seminar, he was starting to get worried that he would have to concede his position. Epstein was still halfheartedly fantasizing that someone shrewder than him would unearth a mistake in the argument, when Gans rose from the back of the room.

The mathematical computation was off, Gans announced.

He pointed out that, with deference to the speaker, the real statistic was even higher, and the code was even less likely to be random than the speaker had said.

Mustering what remained of his skepticism, Epstein and his brother-in-law Dennis Berman, a builder and real estate developer who also attended the seminar, hired Gans to investigate the codes.

Gans verified the mathematical conclusions without delay. It took a year, however, before he was able to undertake his pet project — redoing the 19-day rabbi/yahrtzeit experiment himself, using his own program, which differed radically from Witztum's.

In April, 1989, he began running the 44-hour experiment. But midway through the computer run, as his 386-computer chewed through the 78,064 character Book of Genesis for perhaps the 500,000th time in its search for all the possible pair combinations, the results were already obvious from the print-out sheets spewing from his small printer. Witztum's awesome experiment was correct, down to the finest details.

"It sent a chill up my spine," Gans said, "I had already been fully convinced of the codes' validity before the experiment, but this was electrifying."

Meanwhile, across the ocean, others were also impressed by the research.

Daniel Michaelson, a non-religious professor of math at Hebrew University of Jerusalem, donned a *yarmulke* and became Orthodox after examining the codes discovered by Professor Ely Rips, who worked at Hebrew University, independently of Witztum. Like Gans, Michaelson has since decided to explore codes himself.

Codes research began as a hobby for a brilliant young man in Czechoslovakia in the pre-World-War II era. Rabbi Michoel Dov Weissmandel, better known for his exhaustive efforts to save Hungarian Jews in the holocaust, was a prodigy in astronomy and mathematics as well as Judaic studies. In his youth, he came across an obscure reference to the existence of an equidistant letter code (for example, using every 10th letter of the text) in the Torah, mentioned in the writing of Rabbeynu Bachyah, a 14th-century rabbi.

Rabbi Weissmandel knew from Jewish tradition that there are thousands of ways to translate the Torah, beyond the literal reading of the text. He concluded that equidistant letter codes must be one such "Torah language" and set out to find more examples.

He found codes of stunning beauty, said Rabbi Ezriel Tauber, a former student of Rabbi Weissmandel. Rabbi Weissmandel found dozens, perhaps hundreds, of codes, all without the aid of a calculator or computer.

"How did he count?" Rabbi Tauber asked rhetorically. "When he was young, as a hobby, he wrote out the entire Torah on cards, with 100 letters on each card: 10 rows with 10 letters each. And with that, he counted."

Curiously, Rabbi Weissmandel himself never wrote down his discoveries, though his students did. He saw codes as just another fascinating example of the divine authorship of the work, hardly surprising to a traditionalist. He probably never imagined that years later his codes would convince thousands of non-believing Jews that the Torah is divine.

Epstein never imagined it either.

After Gans' quarterly reports back to Epstein concluded that the codes were fact, Epstein and his wife koshered their kitchen.

"There was no reason for us to have done that if men wrote the Torah," he said frankly. "Would you do it just because some men 3,000 years ago said to do it? Come on."

He also went back to Discovery three more times, for a total of six visits. The last three times he went to take friends — not to punch holes in the argument — because he had found something he wanted them to experience.

And he did something he hadn't dreamed of doing in years. He began studying Torah regularly, twice weekly with two different rabbis.

"After looking under every rock and turning it over and not being able to find anything wrong, I had to consider the evidence as it is. And that got me very interested in Torah," he said.

"If we believe the Torah was written as a message to the world, and not just the world, but even more interestingly, to us specifically as Jews, then you start looking into it with a new, deeper appreciation."

Ultimately, it brought him to the realization that G-d does exist. "He existed anyway," Epstein said. "The only trouble was, I didn't know it."

Codes presentations can be seen around North America as part of the Discovery Seminar by the Aish HaTorah College of Jewish studies. The seminar attracts Jews of all ages and backgrounds. The aim of the seminar is to provide an intellectually satisfying answer to the question, "Why be Jewish?" "Codes" is one class in a mosaic of lectures, workshops, question and answer sessions and social get-togethers that comprise the weekend seminar. In some areas, Discovery is also available in a one-day format.

For information contact:
  Aish HaTorah/Discovery Center
  1388 Coney Island Ave.
  Brooklyn, NY 11230
  Tel: (718) 377-8819
  Fax: (718) 377-8978.

For other learning opportunities contact:
  Jewish Renaissance Center
  210 West 91st Street
  New York, NY
  Tel: (212) 580-9666

  Jewish Learning Exchange (JLE)
  39 Broadway, Suite 3300
  New York, NY 10006
  Tel: (212) 344-2000
        1-800-431-2272
  Fax: (212) 425-7941.

GLOSSARY

BAIS HAMIKDASH: The Temple in Jerusalem (the second of which was destroyed by the Romans in 70 C.E.).

BAIS MIDRASH: Literally, house of learning.

BIYAS HAMOSHIACH: The coming of the Messiah.

BORUCH HASHEM: Blessed is G-d; thank G-d.

CHALAL: Hollow, a void.

CHESSED: Giving, loving-kindness, altruism.

CHILUL HASHEM: Desecration of G-d's name.

CHUTZPAH (Yiddish): Audacity, gall.

DEVARIM: The Book of Deuteronomy.

ERETZ YISROEL: The land of Israel.

HALACHA: Jewish law.

HASHEM: G-d; literally, "The Name."

HASHKAFA: (Torah) outlook.

HASKAMA: Approbation.

KIDDUSH HASHEM: Sanctification of G-d's name.

KOSHER: Dietary laws of the Torah.

LEHAVDIL: As distinct from; no comparison; not to literally compare.

MESHUGA (Yiddish): Crazy.

MIDRASH: Compositor of the (originally) oral homiletical interpretations of Torah whose primary focus is the moral, ethical teachings of Judaism.

MISHNAH: The pithy statements of Jewish law upon which Talmudic discussion is centered.

MITZVAH (MITZVOS pl.): A commandment. The written Torah enumerates 613.

MITZVOS: See *Mitzvah*.

MOSHIACH: Messiah.

NESHAMA: Soul

SHABBOS: The Sabbath.

SHECHINAH: The Divine Presence.

SHEVA BERACHOS: (Literally, "the seven blessings".) The week of festivities following a Jewish wedding.

TALMUD: The oral law transmitted first by G-d to Moses at Mount Sinai and then down through the generations until persecution warranted it being written in the form of the *Mishnah*, and then later on in the form of the *Talmud* as we have it today.

TEFILLEN: The black leather straps and boxes which the Torah commands Jewish men to wear.

TORAH: Scripture (the written Torah) and *Talmud* (the oral Torah) comprising the basic source and essence of Judaism.

YARMULKE: The head-covering worn by Jewish men.

YESHIVA: A school for teaching Torah.

YOM SHEKULO SHABBOS: The day (i.e. era) that is entirely Sabbath.

YOM TOV: Jewish holiday; festival.

ZOHAR: Sourcebook of Jewish mysticism, attributed to Rabbi Shimon bar Yochai (circa 120 C.E.).

REFERENCES

1. Proverbs 3:18.
2. Thus, for instance, the first two of the ten commandments are said in the first person: "*I* am G-d . . ." "You shall have no other gods before *Me* . . ." See also Exodus 20:16, Deuteronomy 4:9,10,12,13,15.
3. See part II. See also <u>To Become One</u>, chapter 4; and <u>I Shall Not Want</u>, chapter 3 and 4 (both books by the author), the idea that the purpose of *hishtadlus* is to reveal G-d's hand in everything we do, including working for a living.
4. Numbers 12:3.
5. Deuteronomy 34:10.
6. See also the subsection ahead entitled *Disciples to the Master Artist.*
7. See <u>I Shall Not Want:</u> *The Torah Outlook On Working For A Living.*
8. See <u>To Become One:</u> *The Torah Outlook On Marriage*, especially chapter 3.
9. Deuteronomy 30:19.
10. Technology is one example of a means to material comfort that much of the world tends to worship as an end. However, communism and even high culture (two of the most 'idealistic' movements at the turn of the century) also fall into the same category. The communistic ideal sounds nice — communal sharing, economic equality, working for the common good, etc. — but the bottom line is that money is its god, i.e, communism's assumption is that if the wealth is distributed evenly then all human avarice will fall away. Ironically, in this sense, communism is no different from the theoretical rival it tried to overthrow, capitalism, in that it saw everything as revolving around economics. Similarly, German/European culture — high culture — made a god out of materialism with its emphasis on the beauty of 'form,' whether that form was literature, poetry, music, theater, etc. The message — the substance — was really secondary. Not surprisingly, later derivations of this movement (nihilism [even Naziism], abstract art, etc.) proudly stood up and declared that the message is that there is no message! (Even when the art form was intended to

convey a true and meaningful deeper message, it never demanded the audience to change. Theater, opera, art and the like create a spectator mentality, expecting its onlookers to applaud, but not change. Torah living, by contrast, is a discipline which demands each individual perform *mitzvos* and become an insider to the knowledge of Torah — in effect to become actual players, each and every individual, on a day to day basis, twenty-four hours a day.) The point is that when people lack or lose sight of the true goal, their indulgence in the disembodied means fosters decadence and breeds despots. They are no longer merely neutral means. — Y.A.

11. *Avos* 1:13.
12. See <u>To Become One</u>, chapter 2, *The Five Levels of Creation*.
13. You open up Your hand and satisfy all the living (Psalms 145:16); In the *Talmud* it is worded: One's entire sustenance for the upcoming year is determined on Rosh Hashannah. (*Baitzah* 16a); see <u>I Shall Not Want</u>, especially the final chapter.
14. This is the principle of *hishtadlus* — see <u>I Shall Not Want</u>, chapter 3, *Hishtadlus - Effort*.
15. Proverbs 3:6.
16. And thus one of the underlying messages of the *Hashkafa* 'Dialogue' Series.
17. See Part II, Chapter 3, subsection *The Difference Between Noah and Abraham*; and essay on *Rosh HaShannah*.
18. G-d 'waits' for mankind to use its free will to choose righteousness, rather than imposing it on them Himself, which would not be true righteousness. See Part II, chapter 3, subsection *Hiring the Operator*; and essay on *Rosh HaShannah*.
19. *Derech Hashem* 2:4:2.
20. (Deuteronomy) 30:11,14.
21. *Beraishis Rabbah* 1:5; *Zohar* 1:24a.
22. This is the import of Rashi (the supreme Torah commentator) to Genesis 1:1, s.v. *beraishis bara*. The first word in the Torah, *beraishis*, is an unusual construct. This peculiarity begs an interpretation more wide-ranging than mere translation, Rashi points out. Two other places such a construct is used are Proverbs 8:22 and Jeremiah 2:3. In those two places, the word *raishis* is used as an analogy for Torah and Israel, respectively. Therefore, in the very first word of Torah — in the word which is synonymous with creation, genesis — is hinted the idea that the world was created for two things: Israel and Torah. When

Torah, the Creator's blueprint of creation, flows through the veins of Israel, the human being who uses his free will to serve G-d selflessly, the glory of G-d flows into the world. That is the goal of creation.

23. First by an agent of G-d (Genesis 32:29), and then by G-d Himself (Ibid. 35:10).

24. As indeed symbolized by Jacob's wrestling and ultimately defeating the angel (even though he is called a 'man' see Genesis 32:31 and Judges 13:21) who told him his name was Israel (Genesis 32:26-29). This angel was the representative of evil (*Tanchuma* 8; *Zohar* 1:170a; cf. *Chullin* 91b; *Beraishis Rabbah* 77:2, 78:6).

25. The Moslems accept the 'Old' Testament, however, claim that Ishmael was the true chosen son of Abraham. Although Genesis 21:12 clearly eliminates Ishmael from G-d's chosen: *For in Yitzchak (Isaac) shall your (Abraham's) seed be called*, the Moslems claim that we changed the Scriptures to make it seem as if Isaac was his spiritual heir. Of course, this sham is exposed by the fact that centuries before Islam was founded, the Scriptures were in the hands of the Christians whose Bibles corroborated the fact that it is the Moslem claim which is fabricated. Similarly, the Christians claim to be the 'spiritual' heirs of the mission of Israel. (G-d rejected the sinful Jews and instead chose the 'righteous' Romans.) Yet, by doing so they completely contradict repeated Scriptural exhortations that G-d chose only the 'seed' of Israel (for example, Deuteronomy 7:6, 7:7, 10:15, 14:2; I Kings 3:8; Psalms 33:12, 135:4; Isaiah 14:1, 41:8, 41:9, 43:10, 43:20, 44:1, 44:2, 45:4 — see <u>Awake My Glory</u> by Avigdor Miller, Chapter 6) and that the uncircumcised or eaters of pork cannot possibly be considered in the congregation of Israel (Isaiah 52:1 and 66:17). For the reader interested in pursuing this subject, a good place to begin is the book <u>The Real Messiah</u>, published by NCSY (a branch of the Orthodox Union).

26. Deuteronomy 10:15.

27. Jacob and Esau were twins, similar on the outside, yet worlds apart on the inside. For instance, Jacob sat in tents, and contented himself with true spirituality (Genesis 25:27); Esau was a hunter, accustomed to spilling blood and taking what he wanted (ibid.). Esau scoffed his birthright and was willing to sell it for a bowl of lentils (Genesis 25:33,34). Jacob was

recognizable through his voice, a quality of spirituality and inwardness, while Esau was known for his hands, the organs of manipulation (Genesis 27:22).

28. Isaiah 42:6.

29. From "Concerning The Jews" *Harper's Magazine*, 1899. For an answer to Twain's last question, What is the secret of his immortality? see subsection *A Soul Linked to Eternity*.

30. Non-Jews have seven universal commandments known as the seven commandments of Noah, so-named because they were given to Noah when he left the ark. The commandments of Noah form the general dictates of righteous behavior G-d expects of all mankind. They are: 1) Not to worship idols; 2) Not to curse G-d; 3) To establish a just court system; 4) Not to murder; 5) Not to commit adultery or incest; 6) Not to steal; 7) Not to eat flesh from living animal. (*Sanhedrin* 56a)

31. *Sanhedrin* 90a.

32. The *Midrash* tells us that Esau, in the end, was beheaded and his head rolled into the Cave of Machpelah, where all the righteous Patriarchs and Matriarchs are buried (*Pirkei D'Rabbi Eliezer* 36). Symbolically, the *Midrash* is informing us that Esau's head was in the right place: he spoke of spirituality and ideals. However, his body pursued murder and material fulfillment. In Esau, the spirit and the body were separated. In essence, this is the Christian ideal where everything boils down to belief in their founder. According to Christian dogma, if Hitler genuinely believed in his heart and accepted upon himself the Christian savior a moment before his death, then he is in heaven while the six million he butchered, who died as Jews, are burning in hell.

33. See the last chapter of I Shall Not Want.

34. For the interested reader: Although the names and certain details have been changed, the basic storyline, including this last quote by Cindy, is true.

35. *Midrash Tehillim* 90; Rashi, *Shabbos* 88b; cf. *Anaf Yosef* ibid.

36. *Sanhedrin* 97a.

37. G-d willing, the next book in the Hashkafa Dialogue Series.

38. *Taanis* 9a.

39. For instance, one of the fifty letter codes starts from the *tav* of the word *bereishis,* the first word in the Torah, in the Book of Genesis. Counting every fifteith letter from that *tav,* the word 'Torah' is spelled out. Coincidence? The exact same fifty letter

code is found at the very end of the book of Genesis. Still not convinced? Starting from the *tav* of the word *shemot,* the second word of the book of Exodus (and the Hebrew name by which this book is known), every fiftieth letter also spells the word 'Torah.' Furthermore, 'Torah' is also encoded at a fifty letter interval at the very end of the book of Exodus just like in Genesis. It does not stop there. The same pattern in reverse exists as well at the beginning and end of both the last two of the Five Books of Moses as well. And all this is only a taste.

40. *Beraishis Rabbah* 1:1.

41. *Avos* 4:4.

42. *Avos* 5:1. Nine times in the account of creation is the statement 'and G-d said' used: Genesis 1:3,6,9,11,14,20,24,26,29. The tenth statement is the very first word *beraishis,* 'In the beginning' (*Rosh HaShannah* 32a).

43. Isaiah 11:9.

44. See the essay on Rosh HaShannah for more on this theme.

45. Genesis 1:28.

46. Genesis 6:11.

47. Genesis 11:4.

48. See Part I, chapter 4.

49. Deuteronomy 4:20.

50. *Avos* 4:7.

51. Leviticus 18:5.

52. The Maharal explains why the Hebrew word for law, *halacha,* actually means "going": it is because the world "runs" or is "going" on the fulfillment of Torah law. This means that even the hairsplitting that goes on in the discussion over fine points of a hypothetical situation is important because through it we learn about the will of G-d; we can deduce from it the general principles of truth which we need to run our lives in accordance with His will. By knowing G-d's will, we come to know Him. This is the greatness of learning Torah. [Editor's note: On the tape from which this story is retold, Rabbi Tauber states that, in the merit of explaining the ensuing *halacha,* the soul of the young man should be elevated.]

53. *Avodah Zara* 17a.

54. *Yoma* 86b.

55. The Viznitzer Rebbe (died c. 1930).

56. Psalms 51:5.

57. Genesis 24:1.

58. Rabbenu Bachya, *VaYashev* 38:30.
59. *Shabbos* 118b.
60. Genesis 3:8.
61. Genesis 18:1-8.
62. *Shabbos* 127a.
63. *Hilchos Avodah Zara* 1:3.
64. *Beraishis Rabbah* 42:8.
65. See Part I, chapter 2, subsection *Light and Shadow*.
66. Genesis 1:28.
67. *Yesodei HaTorah* 5:10.
68. Among the books on this subject is an excellent one by Moshe Prager, <u>Those Who Never Yielded</u>. Prager, among others, is devoted to dispelling the misconception that Jews succumbed to the Nazis without any resistance. The greatest resistance was the spiritual resistance. This fact is lost especially to those who undervalue or place no value on the spiritual. See also ArtScroll's <u>Shoah</u>.
69. *Menachos* 43b.

SHALHEVES

Information
and
Tape List

SHALHEVES

WHAT IS SHALHEVES?
Shalheves is an organization centered around the efforts of
Ezriel Tauber. A Torah scholar and businessman, hardly a day
goes by without someone coming into his office, seeking his
advice on a personal matter.

After years of counseling and lecturing upon request, it
became apparent that there were groups of thirsting Jews
with special interests who needed regular classes on the topics
most relevant to them. Shalheves was started as a network of
lectures and classes devoted to groups such as these. Over the
years a large tape and video collection accumulated. Even
after all this, it was apparent that greater services were
needed. That is when the Shalheves (Yarchai Kallah) Seminar
Weekend was devised.

WHAT IS A YARHAI KALLAH?
It is a gathering of people who want to unplug from the static
and noise of everyday life for a few days in order to listen to
words of Torah that inspire and challenge.

WHO ATTENDS A YARCHAI KALLAH?
Men, women, singles, marrieds, college students, professionals,
business people, secular, religious, yeshivish, chassidic, etc.
The seminars are of basically two types — one geared for the
secular and newly religious, and one geared for the religious.

WHAT HAPPENS AT A YARCHAI KALLAH?
A lot of talking, a lot of eating, some sleeping — all fit
around and between a dozen or so power-packed
presentations, covering topics like Marriage, The Definition
of a Jew, and The Meaning of Shabbos, in addition to ideas
like Creation and Its Purpose, Prophecies Materialized in Our
Times, and Hidden Codes in the Torah.

WHO SPEAKS AT A YARCHAI KALLAH?
Rabbi Ezriel Tauber. Rabbi Shimshon Pincus, Rav of Ofakim in Eretz Israel and Rosh Yeshiva of Yeshivas Yerucham. Guest Speakers like Rabbi Shlomo Brevda, and Rabbi Yisrael Rokovsky.

For information contact:

Shalheves
P.O. Box 361
Monsey, N.Y. 10952
(914) 356-3515

The following is a partial listing of tapes in English by Rabbi Ezriel Tauber, including lectures through Summer 1991. We also have a list of tapes in Hebrew and Yiddish, as well as videos. Prices are $3.00 per tape, and $12.00 per video plus shipping and handling. To order or for an updated list write to:

Emunah-Torah-Tapes
P.O. Box 361
Monsey, New York 10952
(914) 356-3515

Audio Tapes — BEGINNERS

Number	Title
75	An Introductory Lecture to Non-Commited Jews
93	Business and Torah
146	For Beginners
165 A & B	The Creation and its Purpose
167	Business and Torah
170	Life after Death
176	Is There Everyday Life?
201	Purpose of Life (Part 1)
202	Mysticism in Everyday Life (Part 2)
203	Mysticism in Everyday Life (Part 3)
241	Who Am I?
250	New Times of Teshuva
269	Should We Isolate or Integrate?
295	Real Life
307	Jewish Concept of Woman
316	The Structure of the Jewish Nation
317	To Appreciate Our Role
323	Should We Plan?
338	The Value of Time
354 A & B	Codes Revealed in the Torah
394	The Definition of "Yehudi"
757 A & B	Creation and its Purpose
758 A	Definition of a Jewish Nation
758 B	The Benefit of Suffering
759 A & B	Torah Concept of Marriage
796	Be a Proud Jew
817 A	Torah Concept of Marriage
817 B	Reliance on Effort
818	The Value of Life
855	Lets represent G-d

Audio Tapes — INTERMEDIATE AND ADVANCED

Number	Title
250	New Time of Teshuva
258 A & B	The Teshuva Prophecy Realized
261	My Only Request of Hashem
266	The Role of Our Mother Rachel
269	Should We Isolate or Integrate?
271	Chanuka 5745
446	Be an Original Jew
517 A & B	The Definition of Truth
518	The Purpose of Creation
519	Yisrael — Fulfillment of Creation
521	Torah and Tefillah — R. Pincus
522	Closing Address — R. Pincus
523	Effort and Bitachon
524	Marriage of Israel and Hashem
543	Responsibility — Collectively and Individually
544	A Happy Life
546	Kiddush Hashem by Women
552	Enrich Your Life
554	Suffering as Currency
557	Should we be Exposed to the World?
558	The Manna of today
566	The Golden Calf
569	Building the Bais Hamikdash with Our Fire
600	Meaning of the Akeidah
603	Decoration to G-d
607	Life in Gan Eden
613	The Woman's Role in the Family
618	The Man's Role in the Family
620	"Male and Female He Created Them"
623	The Woman's Role in Judaism
625	A Happy Jewish Family
630	Fashion
632	Multiple Plans in the Universe
635	The Bush Burning in Fire
640	Life with Confidence
646	Shira Before Torah
648	The Jewish Nation's Responsibility to the World
651	Woman's Role in Building the Bais Hamikdash
654	Belief and Knowledge
659	Be Aware of Our Times
661	Split Your Own Sea
666	Benefits of the Jewish Dietary Laws
670	All Israel has a Share in the World to Come

Audio Tapes in English — INTERMEDIATE AND ADVANCED

Number	Title
678	Rabbi Akiva's Disciples
682	Let's Do and Listen
688	Thank Hashem for Everything
690	Effort of Competition
691	Stay High — Always
695	Parshas Hameraglim
704	I, As a Walking Bais Hamikdash
708	Selfless Love
709	Role of a Jewish Girl
711	Fill in Your Time
714	Remember Us For Life
718	Two Ways of Praying
719	Obtaining Love of Hashem
720	Choose Life
722	Take Yom Kippur with You
737	Love Your Friend as You Love Yourself
740	"Chinuch" — the Real Way
746	Bring Chanukah
752	Love Hashem
753	Discover Yourself
755	Curiosity — Why?
757 A & B	Creation and its Purpose
758 A	Definition of a Jewish Nation
758 B	The Benefit of Suffering
759 A & B	Torah Concept of Marriage
772	An Effective Prayer
777	Fight Amalek
779	Develop Simcha
782	Believing in Hashem
784	Enjoying the Golus
787	To Combat Proudness
789	The Real Simcha
792	The Haman of Today
793	Mordechai and Esther Today
796	Be a Proud Jew
797	Egypt in Our Times
799	The Full Emunah
805	My Share in the World to Come
810	To be High — or Money
817 A & B	Torah Concept of Marriage
819	The Real World
820	Plant Life
821 A & B	The Meaning of Life

Audio Tapes in English — INTERMEDIATE AND ADVANCED

Number	Title
822	Crucial Times of Today
823	Our Days of Moshiach
824	The Development of Man
829	The Essence of Torah
832	The First Principle of Belief
833	One Solution for all Problems
836	A Moment of Life
837	I, as a Messenger
838	For Single Parents
840	Live for the Present
843	Let's Build the Third Bais Hamikdash
845	Let's Care for Each Other
845	Discover Your Wisdom
849	Make Use of Your Intellect
851	Questions and Answers
855	Let's Represent G-d
857	The Meaning of Chesed
858	Life as a Service to Hashem
862	Truth
863	Tranquility
867	What can I Give to Hashem?
869	Let's be Honest
876	Coronate Hashem
878	Make Me King
881	Join Me Totally
883	Do it for Your Name
890	The Meaning of Simcha
893	How Tefillah works
894	The Real Truth
900	Let's Build Am Yisroel
901	Be Aware of Your Duties
902	How is Hashem Telling Me What To Do
903	Definition of Truth and the Essence of Life
904 A & B	Creation and its Purpose
905 A & B	The Torah Concept of Marriage
906	Effort and Bitochon Towards Parnassa
907	Prophecies in Our Times
909 A & B	Sufferings/Tests During the Times of Moshiach
913	Ner Hashem Nishmas Adam
915	Questions and Answers
920	Why are We Hated?
921	Yaakov's Purchase of Esav's Bechorah
926	Me as Hashem's Candle

Audio Tapes in English — INTERMEDIATE AND ADVANCED

Number	Title
927	Money as Eternity
935	Mitzvas Yediah — Emunah
939	Me as a Chanukah Light
943	Veahavta Lereacha Komocha
944	We as Survivors
945	The Meaning of the Image of Hashem
948	Develop the Right Desire
951	Appreciate Your Role
952	Suffering as a Currency
953 A & B	Reliance and Effort
959	Leaving Egypt Today
960	When Children Question Our Values
964	You Cannot Dilute the Truth
966 A & B	Secret Codes in the Torah
967	Prophecies Materialized in Our Times
968	All of Us Have a Purpose
971	How to Generate Simcha
972	Assimilating Whilst Religious
974	Pesach — Purim — Pesach
979	Enthusiasm for Pesach
988	Ahavas Yisroel
993	Yisroel Victorious
995	Carrying Diamonds
977	Every Inch of Life - An Ongoing Bliss to Avodas Hashem
1000	The Value of a Moment
1003	The Meaning of Happiness
1006 A & B	Chinuch, Courage to say No!
1008	Every Moment A Mission To Hashem
1014	Chinuch for Yourself
1018	Search for Happiness
1019	Build Your Bais HaMikdosh
1021	Achievements of Positive Thinking
1023	Turning Sadness into Joy
1028	The Birthday of Moshiach
1029	Is There Freedom of Choice
1030	The Right Chinuch
1031	Chinuch in T'zneus
1033	The Advantage of Elul
1034	Let's Coronate Hashem
1035	I As A Representative of G-d
1039	The Concealed Power in You
1048	My Resolution

Audio Tapes in English — INTERMEDIATE AND ADVANCED

Number	Title
1055	Power of Prayer
1057	My role in Creation
1061	The Mitzvah in Tshuva
1070	Days of Moshiach
1073	Positive Speech
1077	Chessed to Yourself
1082	How to Prepare for Our Times
1093	Finding Strength
1094	Getting Things done
1097	The Definition of Truth
1098	Creation and its Purpose
1099 A & B	The Torah Concept of Marriage
1100 A & B	Golus, Benefit of Suffering
1102	Depth of Tfillah
1106	Finding Hashem in Business
1107	How to Accept a Loss in the Family
1119	Finding Strength
1120	Sensitivity to Peoples' Needs
1128	Our Crucial days
1129	Our Life as a Plant
1133	How to Wait for Moshiach
1135	Appreciate Being Chosen
1136	Our Times in Depth
1142	Times for Action
1148	Honoring Parents
1149	What are we Really Waiting For?
1153	Waiting for Moshiach
1154	Value of a Moment of Life
1157	My Share in Moshiach
1159	How is Amalek Effecting Us
1169	You as an Artist
1170	Leaving Egypt Today
1180	Our Crucial Days
1185	Questions and Answers
1186	My Personal Growth
1190	Questions and Answers
1192	We as Rabbi Akiva's Students
1200	The Gift of Torah
1201	My Share in Torah
1209	Harmony in the Home I
1210	Harmony in the Home II
1211	Remembering
1218	How to Grow Every Minute

Audio Tapes in English — INTERMEDIATE AND ADVANCED

Number	Title
1221	Today's Bais HaMikdash
1223	Believing
1226	Rebuild the Bais HaMikdash
1228	True Value Vs. Symbolic Value
1230	How to Love a Jew
1233	You as a Bais HaMikdash
1236	How Marriage Helps Us Realize Our Potential
1240	Why Loshon Hara
1242	The Ultimate Goal
1243	The Real Free Choice
1246	The Man in Nature

Special Tape Series

Series of lectures for Divorcees
Series of lectures for Childless Couples
Series of lectures for Single Girls
Series of lectures for Widows
Series of lectures for Couples Who Lost A Child

Additional Tapes in English, Yiddish and Hebrew

English:

Shir HaShirim — Tzror HaMor (10 tapes)
Chovos Halevavos (100 tapes complete)
Maharal — Netzach Yisroel (53 tapes)
Tanya (50 tapes)
Derech Hashem (Series of 7 tapes)

Yiddish:

Chovos Halevavos (51 tapes)
Tanya (30 tapes)
Mesilas Yeshorim (8 tapes)
Bechol Derochechah Daihu (10 tapes)
Ramchal — Derech Hashem (12 tapes)
Maharal — Tiferes Yisroel (52 tapes)
Maharal — Netzach Yisroel (25 tapes)
Maharal — Derech Chaim (19 tapes)
Maharal — Geviros Hashem (14 tapes)
Maharal — Nesiv Hatorah (9 tapes)
Maharal — Or Chodosh (4 tapes)

Hebrew:

Chovos Halevavos (86 tapes)
Parshas Hashovua (81 tapes)
Mesilas Yeshorim (25 tapes)
Tefillah (30 tapes)
Ramchal — Mamar HaIkrim (6 tapes)
Ramchal — Derech Etz Chaim (7 tapes)

In addition, we have tapes from the complete Seminars in English, Yiddish and Hebrew. (Series of about 10-12 tapes per Seminar.)

Video-Tapes available in English, Hebrew and Yiddish

1. The Definition of Truth
2. Creation and its Purpose
3. Definition of Life
4. Torah Concept of Marriage
5. Harmony and Peace in the Jewish Home
6. Prophecies Materialized in our Times
7. Codes in the Torah
8. "Golus" — the Benefit of Suffering
9. Panel Discussion — Questions and Answers
10. The Significance of Torah and Tefillah
11. The Meaning of Shabbos
12. Times of Moshiach
13. Effort and Bitochon towards Making a Living
14. Improving
15. Practicality in Day to Day Life

❧   ❧   ❧

Much of the material in *Choose Life!*, as with the material in the first two editions of the *Hashkafa* Dialogue Series, is taken directly from tapes of Rabbi Tauber's lectures. This book was drawn heavily from the following tapes:

84	Our Times
165	Creation and Its Purpose
201	Purpose of Life
202	Mysticism in Everyday Life
176	Is There Everyday Life?
338	The Value of Time
757	Creation and Its Purpose
758	Definition of the Jewish Nation
1039	The Concealed Power in You (see essay on *Rosh HaShannah*)
1101	The Destiny of Life (used as basis for most of Part II)

In addition, the tape on Creation and Its Purpose from seminar #26 was used for this book. In fact, at every seminar this topic is one of the central lectures. Therefore, a tape from the now more than thirty Shalheves Weekend Seminars on Creation and Its Purpose would be equally as informative.

Anyone interested in extending or reinforcing the material in *Choose Life!* would do well to begin by listening to any or all of the tapes listed here. Also, Rabbi Tauber frequently gives lectures and seminars nation-wide and even world-wide. We encourage letters and inquiries for any information with which we can help you or your group make use of the resources we have available at Shalheves.

Shalheves
P.O. Box 361
Monsey, New York 10952
(914) 356-3515

The *Hashkafa* Dialogue Series

"Where Torah talk is more than just a matter of discussion"

Based upon the tapes and lectures of HaRav Ezriel Tauber, each title in the series is dedicated to presenting the Torah outlook, *hashkafa,* in an inspiring and readable way. It is hoped that, with that with the help of *Hashem,* the content and design will appeal to both the beginning student of Torah as well as the most advanced, so that all who read it will be inspired and encouraged to better use that outlook as a practical guide to everyday living.

Loneliness, confusion, silence—sadly and ironically, these are adjectives too often associated with marriage, the institution designed to unburden men and women of these conditions. Rather than a forum for the most noble emotions and aspirations, to many it is a prison of lost opportunity and failure.

- Are there marriages beyond hope? How do I find fulfillment in marriage?
- Do opposites really attract? What is in my hand to change and what is not?
- What is the purpose of marriage? Are there underlying principles to the numerous statements which the sages made relating to marriage?

To Become One is the real-life dialogue (fictionalized) of a couple seeking answers to these questions, as well as many others.

Genesis 2:24

"Therefore, a man leaves his father and mother, attaching to his wife for them *to become one.*" The secret to successful marriage is contained in this verse, and those who uncover the secret can improve their relationship immediately. In fact, that is how Rabbi Ezriel Tauber has been helping couples for over three decades who have sought his guidance. Contained in these pages, in dialogue form, is the formula he has used to help turn around marriages of all types, even ones that were unhappy for over twenty years!

His method is simple: Explain the root principles of the Torah ideal in order to empower others to grow into fulfilled individuals. By explaining the roots, he shows us how the branches, twigs, and leaves of our personal situations are really a single connected whole. All this makes *To Become One* a unique blend of the practical and the abstract. Read it. Enjoy it. And grow from it.

ISBN 1-878999-01-X